Handbook
of Sacraments
for Today's
Catechist

- ❧ *Covers all seven Sacraments*
- ❧ *Practical activities*
- ❧ *Age-appropriate explanations*

JOYCE SPRINGER

Liguori

ONE LIGUORI DRIVE
LIGUORI MO 63057-9999

This book is dedicated to my wonderfully supportive husband, Bob, who continually encouraged me to share my experience and ideas in writing this book.

....

Imprimi Potest: Thomas D. Picton, CSsR
Provincial, Denver Province, The Redemptorists

Nihil Obstat: Reverend Monsignor Glenn D. Gardner, JCD, Censor Librorum

Imprimatur: † Most Reverend Kevin J. Farrell, DD, Bishop of Dallas,
December 1, 2010

The *Nihil Obstat* and *Imprimatur* are official declarations that the work contains nothing contrary to Faith and Morals. It is not implied thereby that those granting the *Nihil Obstat* and *Imprimatur* agree with the contents, statements or opinions expressed.

Published by Liguori Publications
Liguori, Missouri 63057
To order, call 800-325-9521, or visit www.liguori.org.

Library of Congress Cataloging-in-Publication Data

Springer, Joyce.
   Handbook of sacraments for today's catechist / Joyce Springer.—1st ed.
     p. cm.
   ISBN 978-0-7648-1946-9
   1. Sacraments—Catholic Church—Study and teaching. 2. Christian education of children. 3. Catholic Church—Education. I. Title.
   BX2200.S66 2011
   234'.16—dc22

                                         2010041565

Liguori Publications, a nonprofit corporation, is an apostolate of the Redemptorists. To learn more about the Redemptorists, visit Redemptorists.com.

Printed in the United States of America
15 14 13 12 11   5 4 3 2 1
First edition

CONTENTS

ACKNOWLEDGMENTS

I would like to express my gratitude to the many people who saw me through the writing of this book.

I would like to first and foremost thank my husband, Bob, who supported and encouraged me in spite of all the time this book took me away from him.

I would like to thank my mom, dad and family, who nurtured me in my faith, which led to my lifelong catechetical ministry.

I would like to thank my sisters, Janice and Jeannette, members of the School Sisters of Notre Dame, who have "tested" my creative activities over the years in the classrooms where they have taught and who encouraged me during my writing of this book.

I would like to thank my friends, Julie Buchanan and Janet Harris, who collaborated, read, and offered comments on the content of the book.

Last and not least: I thank those people too numerous to mention who have fashioned me into the catechist and educator I am.

1

SACRAMENTS: GOD'S SPECIAL GIFTS

Sacraments are gifts from God. They are both given and received. Catholics all across the world have the opportunity to open themselves to these sacramental gifts, and just as we receive gifts from God, we also enjoy gifts from loved ones. A well-timed gift can mean everything to a friend or family member.

Can you remember the best gift you ever received? What made it so special? Was it something extravagant or something simple? The truth is, whether the gift is wrapped in a fancy box or whether it is given in a paper sack, it is the meaning and love behind the gift that really counts.

God has given us these gift-giving opportunities because he loves each of us deeply, just as your friends and family love you. Because of this love, God sent his Son, Jesus, as the greatest gift. Jesus is not the only gift that God has given to us. Each of the sacraments is a special gift, given with the love of God. In the sacraments, the Holy Spirit is at work in the Church, showing us the great masterworks of God.

Theology

According to the *National Directory for Catechesis (NDC)*, "the liturgical life of the Church revolves around the sacraments, with the Eucharist at the center." The Church celebrates seven sacraments: baptism, confirmation, Eucharist, penance, anointing of the sick, holy orders, and matrimony. "The sacraments are efficacious signs of grace, instituted by Christ and entrusted to the Church" by which divine life is given to us and celebrated." (*Catechism of the Catholic Church [CCC]* 1131)

We live our lives in the midst of signs and symbols, some of which we create and others that are given to us. Every word we speak and every gesture we make is a sign or symbol that communicates our message to someone.

A sign, usually a simpler concept, generally has one meaning, such as a road sign showing the name or number of the highway on which we are driving.

A symbol usually has more dimensions than a sign and therefore is more complex. Symbolic activity is human activity at its best. When people gather, they often do things of a symbolic nature. Celebrations such as birthdays, holidays, and weddings are examples of these symbolic activities. Rituals belong to symbolic activities.

Formal, ritual activities or celebrations are called sacraments in the Catholic Church. Sacraments point to what is sacred, significant and important for Catholics. God's grace is experienced at these special occasions.

The term "sacrament" comes from the classical and early Latin word *sacramentum*, which means a "sign of the sacred." In order to understand its meaning fully, we need to know that from ancient Greece comes a term known as *mysterion*. Whenever people sensed the presence of a higher power or divinity, then that experience was called *mysterion*. In the Hebrew Scripture and in the Gospels and letters of the New Testament, the term is commonly used.

Tertullian was the first to expand the use of the Roman term of *sacramentum* to mean the rites connected to the initiation rites of baptism, confirmation, and the Eucharist. Saint Augustine used *sacramentum* in a wider sense, not just for the religious rituals of initiation but also other sacred signs. As time passed, Church authorities distinguished between the sacraments that were ceremonies for Christians, and the sacramentals, which were religious objects used in personal piety.

The number of sacraments has been a topic of discussion. Baptism and the Eucharist were generally accepted as coming directly from Jesus. Most Christian churches accept these two sacraments.

Prior to Vatican II, Catholics viewed all sacraments as rigid. Grace was something that you gained by quantity rather than quality. At the time of Vatican II, several theologians tried to expand the thinking on sacraments. While the Council of Trent named the seven official sacraments, these theologians wanted to stress the fact that in a broader perspective, there are sacramental moments, which are grace-filled.

"The purpose of the sacraments is to sanctify…to build up the body of Christ and, finally, to give worship to God. Because they are signs, they also instruct. They not only presuppose faith, but by words and objects, they also nourish, strengthen, and express it. That is why they are called 'sacraments of faith.'" (*CCC* 1123)

Catechetical Perspective

If you are fortunate enough to be a catechist who prepares children to celebrate a particular sacrament, enjoy the time and special bond that can take place when you help a child become a more involved member of the body of Christ and the parish community.

There isn't a parent or catechist who hasn't heard a child's lament, "Mass is boring!" Of course, as adults, we reply, "You get out of it only what you put into it."

But the reality is that unless we help children "put into it," they often don't know how to best understand the liturgy or any other sacrament. As catechists, we're afforded the opportunity to use their hunger for spiritual connections and turn it into a religious session that makes faith more relevant. Luckily, the gift of God's grace can still happen. Grace is God communicating God's own loving self to us. It is offered as a loving, divine energy that fills our bodies and souls. Grace is free and cannot be earned. It comes from God, but God is active and alive each time we meet with our children in class. Our task as a catechist is to help people realize that God is already present in their lives. While we know that the goal of catechesis years ago had been to pass on a body of facts and information while trying to make students loyal to the Catholic Church, we know today that a child must encounter Jesus Christ. This supersedes the child's relationship with the Church. Let's come to understand our faith in catechesis, celebrate it in liturgy, and then live in peace and justice.

Ritual experiences often help the child to best understand the depth of a sacrament. These rituals lead to a deeper understanding of and commitment to faith. Our atmosphere within our classes should encourage prayer, celebrate ritual, and connect meaning to liturgy.

It is natural for children to ask for clarification when they experience ritual in the classroom and see the same symbols or colors in liturgy. For example, the liturgical colors that we may use on a prayer table in our classroom show up on banners or vestments at liturgy. The child may ask, "Why is there so much purple everywhere?" We have the chance to talk about penance, the liturgical season of Lent, and topics related to the season.

In the classroom, you may bless the children using holy water. The child blesses himself or herself with holy water when he or she enters church. When children go to liturgy, they may see the sprinkling rite and begin to see a connection to the water stories that they hear from Scripture.

As a member of the Church community, we should never be alone in our faith journey. This includes children in our catechetical programs. Think about pairing confirmation candidates with children who will be receiving their first Eucharist. They share a common experience of baptism and a desire to be more involved in the faith community of the Church. If the curricula of two different grades focus on the same topic, it is a great time to put the two classes together for shared ritual. Both will benefit.

This could be another natural time to explore together the "oddities" of the sacraments. For example, did you know that it took the Church several centuries to sort out the number of the sacraments? Did you know that baptism is a prerequisite for all other sacraments? Did you know that reconciliation once required years of fasting and penance? Did you know that any Catholic who is sick may receive the anointing of the sick and not just those who are dying?

Family Connection

❍ **Spelling Bee**—Give your child a list of the sacraments misspelled. Have him look up the correct spelling of each sacrament in his textbook and write the correct spelling next to the misspelled word. Then work with the child until he can remember how to spell each sacrament. While it is important for a child to understand each sacrament, it is also important for the child to know how to spell the names of the sacraments. It is much better to do this activity at home instead of in a classroom with children who may have varying spelling abilities.

❍ **Choose a family service project** to help your children realize they are to live as a sacramental people. Stress that we are to share the love of God with others, especially those less fortunate than we are. This service project could include visits to the local nursing home or to an elderly neighbor who may be lonely, helping to gather food for the poor, and collecting items for poor babies or children at holiday time and at other times of the year.

❍ **Wrap a box with gift-wrap,** wrapping the lid and box separately, so that you can take off the lid without ripping the rest of the paper. Put a picture of Jesus inside the box, preferably a picture of Jesus looking happy or being with children. Talk with your children about some of the gifts they have received in the past. What did they feel when they received these gifts? Then explain to your child that the greatest gift she will ever receive will be found in this box. Then explain how this greatest gift—Jesus—also gave them other gifts to help them throughout life. These are the seven sacraments. Review the names and the purpose of each sacrament with your child.

○ **Ask your child to pick one of the seven** sacraments and write a list of adjectives that she thinks of in connection with this sacrament. Help your child to brainstorm these words, if she has trouble. Then give your child magazines or old books from which to cut out pictures or images that connect with the list of adjectives. If you don't have any magazines or books to cut up, help your child find appropriate pictures on the Internet. On a piece of construction paper, write the name of the sacrament and tape or glue the pictures, or have your child draw pictures on the paper that would connect with the list of adjectives. This activity is designed to give your child a better understanding of the meaning of the sacrament.

CATECHETICAL ACTIVITY NO. 1

Have the children make stained-glass windows depicting symbols for each sacrament. For each child, you will need colored construction paper, black construction paper to outline the window, colored tissue paper, scissors, and glue.

Baptism could be the first window depicting the cleansing water of baptism. A number of images can be used for water. You could also put a baptismal candle and white garment within the stained-glass window.

In the second window, the wine and bread of Eucharist could be the symbols used.

Confirmation is the third window, with a white dove or a red flame symbolizing the Holy Spirit.

The symbol for reconciliation is harder to find, but Jesus as shepherd with a sheep could be appropriate. If you are working with younger children and need to keep it simpler, the sheep alone could be used.

Marriage has several symbols, but two interlocking rings would be a recognizable symbol.

Holy orders could have a stole, chalice, or missal, each representing a different aspect of priesthood. Again, for smaller children, you could just use the chalice.

For anointing of the sick, you want to stress a positive view, so perhaps a cloth-draped cross symbolizing the end to human suffering and anticipation of resurrection. A white flower such as a lily could also be a symbol of future life.

CATECHETICAL ACTIVITY NO. 2

Activity stations representing each of the seven sacraments are set up in the parish hall, church, or various classrooms. Each child is assigned a certain station at which to begin. In order to maintain some semblance of order, the children follow the order of the stations, taking ten minutes per station. Some possible things to do at the stations are:

Music: Listen to a song that is indicative of a particular sacrament. Then sing along with the song, adding appropriate gestures.

Artwork: Make a picture or do a craft project that illustrates the symbols of the sacrament.

Movie clip: Watch a short DVD or a YouTube video showing the celebration of a sacrament.

Act out situation cards: Various situations are written out on cards, and the children have to decide how to live their lives when that situation would come up.

Bible: Read and discuss a Bible story that tells of Jesus curing someone or sharing bread and wine.

Church tour: Talk about the various places where each sacrament is celebrated. For example, the baptismal font is the site of baptism celebrations.

Prayer: Make up original prayers remembering those persons in the parish who are going to be celebrating their sacraments this year.

CATECHETICAL ACTIVITY NO. 3

Print out the name of each sacrament on an index card. Leave plenty of space between the letters on the card because you are going to cut apart each word, letter by letter. Put all letters for each sacrament into an envelope. Give each child a different envelope (seven envelopes with the names of seven sacraments). See how quickly they can figure out which sacrament they have in their envelope and put the letters in correct order to spell out the sacrament. After a certain time, exchange envelopes until each child learns to put the name of the sacrament in correct order. Depending on the age of the children, you may want to have the names of the sacraments written on a poster or board within the classroom.

CATECHETICAL ACTIVITY NO. 4

Match the following descriptions with the names of each sacrament.

1. The sacrament through which the Holy Spirit comes to us in a special way and helps us to profess our faith as a strong Christian
2. The sacrament that gives health and strength to someone who is ill or aged
3. A sacrament that is both a sacrament and a sacrifice
4. The sacrament by which sins are forgiven through the absolution of the priest
5. The sacrament that binds a baptized man and a baptized woman to each other for life
6. The sacrament through which men receive the grace and power to perform sacred duties as bishops, priests, or deacons
7. The sacrament through which we become a child of God and heir of heaven

Answers are shown below in parentheses.

____ Baptism (#7)

____ Confirmation (#1)

____ Eucharist (#3)

____ Reconciliation (#4)

____ Anointing of the sick (#2)

____ Matrimony (#5)

____ Holy orders (#6)

CATECHETICAL ACTIVITY NO. 5

Take a gift bag that you would use for gift-giving at a special occasion. Fill the gift bag with a symbol from each sacrament. Some choices could be: a white cloth to symbolize the white garment used at baptism, a red flame cut from paper or an artificial dove for confirmation, a small loaf of bread for the Eucharist, a key to heaven symbolizing the grace of reconciliation, a small jar with oil for anointing of the sick, some gold rings or chocolate kisses for matrimony, and a cross for holy orders. Have a child pull out one of the symbols from the bag and discuss the symbolism for that particular sacrament. As an additional activity you could have each child put together her own bag of symbols. You may be surprised at how astute the children are.

CATECHETICAL ACTIVITY NO. 6

Scavenger hunts are favorites of children of any age. Hide items around your classroom that show the various symbols of the seven sacraments. You can use some of the same items that are mentioned in Catechetical Activity No. 5 above, or you can choose different symbols. If you have a large number of children in your class, you may want to hide several sets of symbols so that each child can find one or two symbols. Discuss the sacraments and the symbols before beginning the scavenger hunt.

Concluding Remarks

Sacraments are special signs celebrated by the Catholic Church to remind us of God's never-ending love. The more that is learned about the sacraments, the more that a person can celebrate them.

Teaching sacraments is very important in the education of children. Each of the sacraments has a special place in the journey of life, and the way in which these sacraments are taught will influence how the children move through that journey. It will influence how close the children will stay aligned to the Catholic Church. Easy-to-understand family and catechetical activities will enhance the depth of understanding of these special gifts.

2

Baptism, Confirmation, Eucharist and Reconciliation for Children in Grades Four through Eight

A short story

A young boy is walking on a sidewalk in front of a small pet store when he spots five puppies in the front window. He goes into the pet shop and asks the owner if he can hold the puppies, even though he can't afford to buy one. The pet shop owner agrees and four puppies come running out of the cage, but the last puppy comes limping out. The little boy asks what is wrong with the last puppy. The owner explains that the puppy has a birth defect in his hip socket and that he will never be able to run normally. The little boy asks how much it would cost to buy that puppy. The owner replies "Oh, you don't want to buy that puppy. He will never be able to run and jump and play with you." The little boy pulls $3.15 out of his pocket and says, "No. That is the puppy that I want. I will give you this $3.15 as a down payment, and I'll pay you every week from my allowance until I have paid enough to buy that puppy." The owner again tries to convince the boy that he doesn't want to buy the puppy. He will just give the puppy to the boy free of charge. This makes the boy even more upset. "I don't want you to give me the puppy. He is worth as much as each of the other puppies," the boy responds. The store owner again reminds the boy of the puppy's limitations. Finally, the boy pulls up the leg of his pants to reveal a heavy metal brace. "Well, I don't run so well myself, and this little puppy may need someone who understands."

When we go into our catechetical class, we may not know the challenges and struggles that each child is experiencing. What is most important is that we treat each child as a valuable person, and that we allow each child to be treated with respect. We know how different each child can be from the other children. Yet we love each one for who she is, knowing that she is unique and special in the eyes of God. Our message, both spoken and unspoken, to each child is that he or she is important.

It is often easy to blame the child for something out of his control. For example, each of us as catechists has wanted to judge the child because he has received his first sacraments (baptism, reconciliation and the Eucharist) but doesn't go to Sunday Mass. Yet when checking into the reason, it is obvious that the parents don't go to Sunday Mass, and the child lives too far away to walk on his own. So, instead of blaming the child, we should perhaps look into ways to engage the parents in the faith life of the parish.

Theology

"On another occasion he (Jesus) began to teach by the sea. A very large crowd gathered around him so that he got into a boat on the sea and sat down. And the whole crowd was beside the sea on land. And he taught them at length in parables." (Mark 4:1–2)

Teaching was an integral part of Jesus' ministry on earth. Just as Jesus taught with authority and to all people no matter what their age or walk of life, so he commissioned his disciples to continue his teaching ministry. Our role as catechists is to likewise continue Jesus' teaching ministry, whether that is in a Catholic school or a parish religious education program, our teaching of religion is an essential part of our life as Catholics. We are called to this ministry because of our baptism and because of our willingness to respond to an important need in the life of the Church. "All the baptized, because they are called by God to maturity of faith, need and have therefore a right to adequate catechesis." (*General Directory of Catechesis [GDC],* No. 167)

Children of all ages will come to the parish needing to receive the sacraments. For whatever reason and circumstance, the child may not be on the "usual" schedule of having received the various sacraments. It is our responsibility to offer the opportunity to the child to be catechized in preparation for these sacraments. However, the catechesis for these children will be more like the catechumenate than like traditional religious education classes. In order to bring out the paschal character of baptism, the Easter Vigil is the ideal place to celebrate the sacraments of initiation for these children. If this is not possible, celebration of these sacraments should be done at a Sunday liturgy. "The Church's catechesis—and even more so, the catechist—must take into consideration all the human factors of a particular age level in order to present the Gospel message in a vital and compelling way. From infancy through maturity, catechesis is thus a permanent school of the faith and follows the major stages of life." (*NDC,* No. 48)

Physical, social, and psychological development of the pre-adolescent/adolescent of grades four through eight needs to be taken into account when planning the sacrament preparation classes. Home and family are still important, but peer groups also play a huge part in the development and influence of the young person. In grades four through six, the children care deeply about learning, struggle with loyalty to family versus loyalty to friends, and experience higher rates of moodiness.

In grades seven and eight, young people begin to understand other points of view, experience self-consciousness, value peers, become interested in other faiths, and need strong adult role models.

Pre-adolescence and adolescence are the times of hero worship, so it is especially important to present Jesus and other important Catholic figures in a context where the young person could imitate them. Jesus is a guide, a friend, and a model for the young person. This is the time for formation of behavior, attitudes, and values. They learn to live the Catholic faith by imitating and seeing others living their faith.

Jesus touches our lives through the sacraments. When we celebrate the sacraments, these are signs of Jesus' presence in our lives. We receive grace each time we celebrate the sacraments. While we are preparing children to receive the sacraments of baptism, reconciliation, the Eucharist, and confirmation, it is still important to give the children an overview of all seven sacraments.

The sacraments of initiation lay the foundation. In baptism we receive new life in Christ. Baptism takes away original sin and gives us new spiritual birth. The sign of baptism is the pouring of water. In confirmation we seal our life of faith in Jesus. Confirmation increases and deepens the grace of baptism. Like baptism, confirmation is received only once. The signs of confirmation are the anointing with oil and the laying on of hands, usually by a bishop. In the Eucharist, our life of faith is nourished as we receive the Body and Blood of Christ. The signs of Eucharist are the bread and wine that are changed into the Body and Blood of Christ.

The sacraments of healing celebrate the healing power of God. In reconciliation, we receive God's forgiveness and healing grace when we confess our sins to a priest and receive absolution. The signs of reconciliation are the confession of our sins and the words of absolution.

In anointing of the sick, a sick or aged person unites his suffering with the suffering of Jesus. Strength and grace are received. The sign of this sacrament is the anointing with oil.

The sacraments at the service of communion are those that confer a mission in the Church that serves the people of God. In matrimony, a baptized man and woman join with each other in marriage promises. The signs of this sacrament are the wedding rings, and the couple themselves minister the sacrament. In holy orders, men are ordained and consecrated as deacons, priests, or bishops. Each degree of ordained ministry, in ways particular to the degree, shares in Jesus' ministry of teaching, sanctifying, and building the Church. The signs of this sacrament are the anointing of oil by the bishop and the laying on of hands.

Catechetical Perspective

One of the greatest challenges you will have as a catechist in working with children of older ages in preparation for first sacraments is that you don't know what the children have previously learned. If you have ten children in the class, they literally could have ten different amounts of knowledge on any religious topic. Therefore start by asking the students to answer the following questions:

❍ What do you know about God?
❍ Who is Jesus?
❍ What do you know about the Holy Spirit?
❍ Do you know what book God inspired?
❍ What Bible story do you remember?
❍ What is your favorite story about Jesus?
❍ Who was Jesus' mother?
❍ Do you know the names of any of the sacraments?
❍ What do you know about going to Mass?
❍ What prayers do you know?

One way to help each of the children learn as much as possible in a "sacrament prep" class is to create a book titled "Things We

Believe About Our Religion." Ideas for six chapters in the book are listed below, but you could add more chapters if your class goes longer.

Week one for the book
Talk about the people within the church: pastor, bishop, etc. Try actually to meet the priest, deacon, religious sister, and/or other parish staff members. Write a story in the book about one of the people that you met.

Week two for the book
How do Catholics pray? Include in the book the Sign of Cross, the Our Father, the Hail Mary and Glory Be. Make a door knocker with each prayer so the students can practice each prayer at home.

Week three for the book
Study the basics of baptism. Discuss the signs of baptism (color of white, candle, water, oil and sign of cross). Take a trip to church to see the baptismal font. Discuss the gifts of baptism (welcome into the Church, become child of God, Jesus becomes your brother, Holy Spirit dwells in you, receive God's graces, freedom from original sin, gates of heaven are open) and write them in the book. Then have the students make a box and write on the box the different gifts received at the time of baptism. Write their favorite gift on a piece of paper that they put into the box and then wrap the box in pretty paper.

Week four for the book
Study the basics of confirmation, including the signs of confirmation (color of red, fire, oil, and laying on of hands). Study the gifts of the Holy Spirit and write these gifts in the book. Then have the students draw a picture of a fruit bowl, putting a gift on each piece of fruit. If possible, have them bring a bowl to class and make fruit pieces out of papier-mâché. With a marking pen, write the gift on

the fruit piece. The recipe for the papier-mâché paste is below in the catechetical activity section.

Week five for the book
Study the basics of the Eucharist. In their book, draw pictures of the bread and wine. Discuss how Catholics worship. Go to Mass after this study. Put together a separate Mass booklet using pictures and words, outlining what happens at the Mass.

Week six for the book
What do Catholics believe? Study the Apostles' Creed line by line. Make sure that each of the students understands what he is believing. In the book write the Apostles' Creed.

Family Connection

○ **Send copies of the prayers** to the families so they can work on the prayers at home. This should be done in the home, where the parents are the primary religious educators of the child.

○ **Get a children's Bible** and read a Bible story to your children regularly. Each child should be able to retell his favorite Bible story.

○ **Mentally go through each room** in your house. How Catholic is it? What religious articles do you have in the home? Do you have a particular place as a prayer corner? Do you have a crucifix anywhere in the home? Do you have a statue of Mary?

○ **Make a Christ candle** to light in the home on special occasions. This is a candle that is blessed by a priest and could have a cross carved or pasted on it. Crayons or markers could also be used to draw the cross on the candle. The Christ candle mirrors the paschal candle that is a symbol of the risen Christ. Just as Jesus was released from the tomb, so we are released from the bonds of sin and given new life.

○ **At least once a week at dinner,** share a fun question with your children to spark conversation. For example, if you had to describe your personality as one of the four seasons, which one would you choose and why?

CATECHETICAL ACTIVITY NO. 1

Do an art project on a Catholic belief or Bible story. For example, divide the paper into six "windows" and create a page on the various days of creation. Use a large piece of poster board for this project. You could also make mobiles of each day of creation to hang in her room at home.

CATECHETICAL ACTIVITY NO. 2

Do an in-depth study of the saints. Explain to the students that these people followed Jesus and became holy because of the way they lived their lives. Through the formal process in the Catholic Church called canonization, these holy people are named saints. Saints serve as models of holiness for us and intercede to God when we pray to them.

In studying the lives of the saints, here is one possible process:

❍ Identify the saint the student wants to study.
❍ Research the life of the saint through the Internet and through books of the *Lives of the Saints*.
❍ Write a short biography of the saint's life. Be sure to include what he or she did to follow Jesus.
❍ If possible, find medals or holy cards of that saint. If there are none available, make a holy card of the saint.
❍ Identify some trait or virtue that the saint demonstrated and that the student could imitate. Discuss why it is important to follow the saint's example.
❍ Ask the students to share the life of their saint with a family member, neighbor, or friend.

CATECHETICAL ACTIVITY NO. 3

Here is a recipe for no-cook papier-mâché paste that can be used with a class. It is easy to make. Materials needed are water and flour.

Instructions: To make this papier-mâché paste, mix together one part flour to two parts water. You will want it to be the consistency of thick glue, but you also want it to be runny and not thick like paste. Add more water or flour as necessary. Mix well to remove any lumps.

Here are a few helpful tips for using this paste:

○ If you live in an area with high humidity, add a few tablespoons of salt to help prevent mold.
○ If you don't like the smell of the glue mixture, add a few sprinkles of cinnamon to sweeten it.
○ You should be able to store this glue in a covered bowl or jar, in the refrigerator, for a few days.

CATECHETICAL ACTIVITY NO. 4

Find an old (or previously used) catechetical textbook that has the pictures and outline of what happens at Mass. Take the pictures and cut them apart. Mount these pictures on larger poster board pieces. Give each student a picture and have the class arrange the pictures in the order of what happens at Mass. If you have a large number of students, form two groups and race to see which one can put its Mass in the correct order first.

CATECHETICAL ACTIVITY NO. 5

On a large sheet of paper, write the word "God" on one side of the paper, filling most of the paper with the word. Color the paper. On the other side of the paper write the word "Love," filling most the paper with the word. Color that side of the paper. Cut the sheet of paper into several pieces, like a puzzle. Have the students put the puzzle together, showing that if we seek God, love will follow in our lives.

CATECHETICAL ACTIVITY NO. 6

In order to illustrate the unique gifts of each student, bring to class a fish net or fish bowl filled with paper fish of all sizes and shapes. Have the students pick a fish from the net, color it and put their names on it. As you can imagine, each one will be a "one-of-a-kind" fish. Over the course of the year, hand-write each student a note telling the student why you are glad that you have that student in your religion class. Praise the student for one particular quality.

CATECHETICAL ACTIVITY NO. 7

Because of the age of the older students, service projects should be a part of preparation for the sacrament of confirmation. This is a tangible part of the Church's social teaching. It is important to reflect on the service project, in order to be fully effective.

First determine the "who," "what," "how," and "why" of the service situation. This step attempts to understand the reasons the current condition exists.

The second step is to find insights from the faith tradition as to how a person of faith would respond to the current condition.

The third and final step is to take action. This is the faith-filled response that seeks to address the current condition and improve the situation.

There are dozens of service project possibilities. What is important is that our projects show us how our faith compels us to interact with the world and to put our faith into action.

Be sure the students do not think that they must do service projects in order to "earn" the sacrament of confirmation. Rather, to follow Jesus is to be of loving service to others as Jesus was. Jesus gave us the example of service throughout his life.

Concluding Remarks

When children are older and are learning about the sacraments for the first time, they are more inclined to see them as passages of life. Each of the ceremonies that are part of the sacrament point to what is sacred in Christianity. These ceremonies also provide a means of ritual that enable a smooth and special transition to a deeper love of God and a deeper love of the Catholic Church.

Activities that gently educate these students about these sacraments and ceremonies will give them a better understanding of the importance within their daily faith life.

3

BAPTISM

Being a godparent is a special responsibility and an opportunity to serve as a model for bringing a child to faith through a unique relationship. The godparent and godchild exchange Christmas gifts. The godparent and godchild exchange frequent phone calls and emails. The godparent is a lector at the wedding of the godchild. There is a special bond between godparent and godchild that takes place and is shared at good and bad times of life.

Indeed the special bond that begins at baptism is the beginning of a lifelong close relationship. At the time of baptism the child gets "new" clothing, a candle to light the way, water to help the child grow, oil for strength, and a spiritual companion for the journey.

What are the criteria for choosing a godparent? Do parents look for a relative who helped out during the pregnancy? Do parents look for someone who is actively involved in the Church, no matter whether a friend or relative?

The baptism of your child is a big day that requires some prayer and thought about the choice of the godparents. Godparents are to represent the Church and the Catholic community. And they help the child's parents raise the child in the Catholic Church, so that the child grows up as an active adult in the Church.

What are the requirements for a baptismal godparent? Church law now insists that the person is at least sixteen years old, fully initiated in the Church (by having received the Eucharist and confirmation), be someone other than the parents, and be someone who leads a life in harmony with the Church.

At least one of the two godparents needs to be a committed and active Catholic, although ideally it would be both godparents. "The godfather and godmother…must be firm believers, able and ready to help the newly baptized…on the road of Christian life." (*CCC* 1255) If only one godparent is a committed Catholic, the other godparent can serve as a witness. Ultimately, the responsibility to raise this child in the Catholic faith is the responsibility of the entire Catholic parish. "It takes a village," as a popular saying goes.

Theology

Baptism is the first of the sacraments of initiation. Through this sacrament a person is incorporated into the Church, and baptism is the door to the other sacraments. The Eucharist and confirmation are the other two sacraments of initiation. In these other two sacraments, the person is strengthened to participate in the Church's ministry, and the person receives the Body and Blood of Christ.

The practice of baptism was a common rite of initiation and dates back to the early centuries. In the first century, the ancient religions made use of initiation rites, which drew upon Jewish and Christian traditions. The Jews practiced a rite of cleansing at the time of Jesus. By the second century, the Jewish rituals had developed into initiatory rites especially aimed at the Gentiles. Christianity used baptism to express freedom from sin, union with Jesus and the Church, our participation in the death and rising of Jesus, and new life in the Holy Spirit.

In the Eastern churches, baptism, confirmation and the Eucharist are celebrated at one time, usually in infancy. In the Latin church, each of these sacraments is celebrated separately, except in cases of emergency and in cases of RCIA (Rite of Christian Initiation of Adults).

However, at the time of preparation for any of these three sacraments, the parish presents a comprehensive and systematic theology of all of the sacraments of initiation. In the first three centuries of the Church, baptism was aimed at adults. As Christianity spread, adults were encouraged to join the group known as catechumens. This group studied the faith and took a step-by-step process toward joining the Church. This process was short-stepped, however, once Emperor Constantine in 313 allowed people to be baptized upon request.

By the fifth century, infant baptism became the norm. The theology that is presented for the RCIA group is also appropriate for the baptism of infants. The parents and godparents need to reexamine their own lives and how well they are living the Catholic faith. "An infant should be baptized within the first weeks after birth." "If the child is in danger of death, it is to be baptized without delay." (Rite of Baptism of Children, No. 8)

As Catholics we believe that baptism imprints on our souls an indelible mark that marks us forever as Catholics. Any stain of original sin (the sin that is imparted to all people because of the fall of Adam and Eve) is gone with baptism. The child receives sanctifying grace, which is God's life within us. The child is anointed to become part of a community of believers known as the mystical body of Christ on earth.

Baptism is the Church's way of celebrating and enacting God's love, which had been in existence from the moment of conception. Baptism is a ritualization of becoming a temple of the Holy Spirit and of the child's desire to be a child of God. Baptism is much more than the moment of celebration. At the time of baptism the parents and godparent are asked: "What do you ask of God's Church?" The answer is, "faith!" Faith must grow after baptism. The child grows into being a son or daughter of God. The child's family and the child's church community help him take those steps to grow.

A bishop, a priest, or a deacon usually ministers baptism. However, in case of emergency, any person (even someone not baptized) can baptize as long as he has the required intention. This means that the person performing the baptism follows the form of baptism, and intends, by the baptism, to do what the Church does in bringing the person being baptized into the fullness of the Church. This person would pour water over the head of the person being baptized while saying: "I baptize you in the name of the Father, and of the Son, and of the Holy Spirit." A priest may later perform a conditional baptism.

With respect to children who have died without baptism, the liturgy of the Church invites us to trust in God's mercy and to pray for their salvation. (*CCC* 1283)

Besides the baptism with water, there are two other types of baptism: baptism of desire and baptism of blood. Baptism of desire applies to those who die before receiving the sacrament, while wishing to be baptized. This would include those studying as catechumens to be baptized and/or those who through no fault of their own do not know of the Church. Baptism of blood refers to the martyrdom of those believers who were killed for the faith before they had a chance to be baptized.

Catechetical Perspective

The first sacrament Jesus gave us is baptism. All four Gospels make reference to Jesus' baptism, although it is less direct in the Gospel of John. John the Baptist baptized Jesus in the Jordan River, although Jesus was without sin and thus received a non-sacramental baptism. Jesus wanted to show how important baptism is for everyone.

The baptized were to leave the bondage of sin and live in the freedom of the spirit in the Promised Land. Jesus proclaimed his relationship as son to God the Father in his baptism. In all Gospels but John's, God addresses either Jesus or the crowd affirming his pleasure with Jesus. "You are my beloved Son; with you I am well pleased" (Luke 3:22). Just as Jesus is God's son, baptism makes each of us a son or daughter of God. We are to live and follow in the footsteps of Jesus who, after his baptism, went out teaching and healing and preaching the Good News.

All three synoptic Gospels stress the role of the Holy Spirit as the greatest gift of baptism. Jesus told his twelve apostles to "go out and make disciples of all nations, baptizing them in the name of the Father, and of the Son, and of the Holy Spirit." (Matthew 28:19)

In the Gospel of John, two baptism stories particularly stand out. When Jesus encountered Nicodemus (John 3:1–21), Jesus made it very clear that baptism was necessary for salvation: "Amen, amen I say to you, no one can enter the kingdom of God without being born of water and spirit" (verse 5). The second story is the man born blind found in John 9:1–41. Jesus sends the man to go and wash in the pool of Siloam, after having smeared clay on the man's eyes. Because Siloam means "the one sent," the blind man is to wash himself in the person of Jesus.

As Jesus approached his passion and death, Jesus added another dimension to the idea of baptism. Being baptized includes the dimension that the person is willing to suffer and die for the sake of the kingdom. Jesus said: "There is a baptism with which I must be baptized, and how great is my anguish until it is accomplished." (Luke 12:50)

In another Gospel, Jesus stresses the need for the baptism of "new" life in his reprimand to James and John. They are requesting to sit at Jesus' right and his left in the kingdom. Jesus reminds them "You do not know what you are asking. Can you drink the cup that I drink or be baptized with the baptism with which I am baptized?...The cup that I drink, you will drink, and with the baptism with which I am baptized, you will be baptized." (Mark 10:38–39)

In the Acts of the Apostles, we find that the heart and soul of baptism is rooted in the belief of Jesus. We hear the story of the conversion of Saul to Paul as an example. Baptism is never a private matter. While baptism is a grace-filled act of God with the person being baptized, the community of believers is central to the understanding of the mission that is a part of baptism.

In Paul's letters we begin to see a more developed theology and understanding of baptism. Through baptism believers share the death of Christ and escape from the grip of sin. Saint Paul asks the early believers: "Are you unaware that we who were baptized into Christ Jesus were baptized into his death? We were indeed buried with him through baptism into death, so that, just as Christ was raised from the dead by the glory of the Father, we too might live in newness of life." (Romans 6:3–4) Baptism marks the end of the power of sin. The believer lives a new kind of life for God, with whom he is united. Baptism communicates the life-giving power of the risen Lord.

The sacrament of baptism is multi-faceted. In baptism, our sins are washed away, and we become children of God and members of the Church. Baptism gives us a special gift, or grace, to believe in God, to love him, and to grow in goodness. Once we have been baptized, we have an important new job for the rest of our lives: to tell others about the love of Jesus.

In some parishes, infant baptisms are celebrated during the Sunday liturgy. It is a time when the community of believers gather and join in the celebration. It is also a reminder that each time someone is baptized, she becomes a member of our church community.

Water is the obvious symbol of baptism. Water refreshes, cleanses, and gives life. It represents freedom from death and new life. Water can also take away life. In baptism the person dies to all that is not of Christ: "We were indeed buried with him through baptism into death, so that, just as Christ was raised from the dead by the glory of the Father, we too might live in newness of life." (Romans 6:4)

The chrism oil is another symbol. It is used within the baptismal ceremony and represents the anointing of the newly baptized for the mission and ministry of Jesus and of the Church. The white garment reflects the light and symbolizes newness. The baptismal candle lit from the community's larger Easter candle symbolizes the fire of the Holy Spirit.

Family Connection

○ **Look up the dates** of everyone's baptism. Post these on a calendar. Celebrate the baptismal date with a special meal or gift for each person.

○ **The sacrament of baptism is conferred** "in the name of the Father and of the Son and of the Holy Spirit." Just as God's name sanctifies each person, names chosen for the child at the time of baptism signify a tie to a saint, a virtue or Christian mystery. While parents may choose a name that is not a saint's name, the name must not be offensive to Christian values. Baptismal names are important. My baptismal name includes "Anne" after my mom and after the grandmother of Jesus. As a family, talk about each person's baptismal name. Why was the particular name chosen for each person?

○ **The feast of the Baptism of Jesus** (the first Sunday after Epiphany) is a wonderful day to remember our baptismal vows and to celebrate the gift of baptism that God has given to us. Invite your child's godparents to come for a visit that day, if geographically possible. Bring out the baptismal gown and the baptismal candle, if you have saved them. Reminisce about the child's baptismal day. Show any photos or video of the day. Have a meal with the family and godparents, if possible. Use the lighted candle as a centerpiece for the table. Say the Apostles' Creed as a prayer, which reminds all gathered of what we believe as Catholics.

○ **Write a parent's prayer or wish** for your child that states how you hope the child will grow up and live a life of Catholic faith. Share your hopes and your dreams.

CATECHETICAL ACTIVITY NO. 1

Get the name or names of any people who are part of the parish RCIA group. Prepare a card welcoming them into the parish community. Mail the cards after Easter, or give them to the people after the Holy Saturday liturgy.

CATECHETICAL ACTIVITY NO. 2

If you or someone you know is familiar with PowerPoint, you could create a slide show about previous celebrations of the sacrament of baptism. You can scan photos taken during the celebration of rites at your own parish (including the Easter Vigil ceremony) and insert them into the presentation. The children in your class may also have photos to bring for scanning from their own baptisms or the baptisms of their siblings.

CATECHETICAL ACTIVITY NO. 3

Humor is often understood by older children, and can be a "teachable moment." This popular story has circulated over the years, bringing back memories of a Catholic Church of long ago. After telling the story, discuss the ways in which the customs of the Catholic Church have evolved over the years. Discuss the importance of living our baptismal promises.

"When Olé quit farming, he discovered that he was the only Lutheran in his new little town of all Catholics. That was OK, but the neighbors had a problem with his barbecuing beef every Friday.

Since they couldn't eat meat on Friday, the tempting aroma was getting the best of them. Hoping they could do something to stop this, the neighbors got together and went over to talk to Olé. 'Olé,' they said, 'since you are the only Lutheran in this whole town and there's not a Lutheran church for many miles, we think you should join our church by becoming a Catholic.'

"Olé thought about it for a minute and decided they were probably right. Olé talked to the priest, and they arranged it. The big day came and the priest had Olé kneel. He put his hand on Olé's head and said, 'Olé you were born a Lutheran, you were raised a Lutheran, and now,' he said as he sprinkled some water and incense over Olé's head, 'now you are a Catholic.'

"Olé was happy and the neighbors were happy. But the following Friday evening at suppertime, there was again the aroma of grilled beef coming from Olé's back yard. The neighbors went to talk to him about this and as they approached the fence, they heard Olé saying to the steak: 'You were born beef, you were raised beef,' and as he sprinkled salt over the meat he said, 'and *now* you are fish.'"

CATECHETICAL ACTIVITY NO. 4

Children remember much more of what they do than what they hear. With younger children, imitate a baptism ceremony with the children taking the parts of the parents, godparents, priest, altar servers, and parish community. A doll can be used for the baby.

CATECHETICAL ACTIVITY NO. 5

As a class, pray the *Litany of the Saints*, which is part of the rite of baptism. Have each child add his or her baptismal saint to the litany, and have everyone respond "pray for us." Be sure to discuss the baptismal saints before praying the litany to make sure that each child knows his particular saint.

Concluding Remarks

The "door of the Church" is the nickname often given to the sacrament of baptism. It is not only the first of the sacraments in time but in priority, since the reception of the other sacraments depends on it. Once baptized, the person becomes a member of the Catholic Church.

It is this relationship that is critical to the catechetical teaching of the child. For most of the children, the baptismal ritual took place during infancy. This was before they could say "yes" on their own. Their parents, godparents and faith community hopefully have followed through on the promises they repeated that day. They came to the waters of baptism already connected to people who cared for and loved them. It is the Gospel of Jesus Christ that holds both the challenges and the answers to how to live their faith. This is the same Gospel of Jesus Christ that is central to the catechetical lessons.

4

CONFIRMATION

Do you remember when you were confirmed? Some people were confirmed at young ages such as eight or nine years old. The rite of confirmation included being anointed with oil on the forehead, being slapped lightly on the cheek, and singing the song *Come Holy Ghost*. The bishop said a prayer and put his hand on the head of the person being confirmed. There was a feeling of being commissioned as a soldier of Christ.

The role of the confirmation sponsor is to bring the candidates to the sacrament, present the candidates to the bishop for anointing, and help the candidates fulfill their baptismal promises. The sponsor serves as a guide and witness. Ideally the young person's baptismal sponsor should be used as the confirmation sponsor, strengthening the bond between those two initiation sacraments. Sponsors should be at least sixteen years old, be faithful practicing Catholics, and must be fully initiated in the Church.

Today the sacrament is often defined as a sacrament of mature Christian commitment. Many parishes confirm students when they are in junior high or high school. However, some parishes confirm students at the time of first Eucharist, just as there are some children in the Eastern Rite churches who confirm at the time of baptism. The bishops have given a wide range of ages for the reception of the sacrament.

In Scripture, the apostle presiding over the young Church community baptized new members, anointed them with oil, and then gave them the Eucharist for the first time. Each year at the Easter Vigil, adults and some older children receive that same rite of initiation in receiving confirmation immediately after their baptism. At the time of Communion, the newly received members of the Church receive the Eucharist for the first time.

Theology

The history of the sacrament of confirmation is complex, and the theology of the sacrament is equally complex. What we now celebrate is one of the several rites the early Church used to celebrate the gift of the Holy Spirit. Christians were baptized as part of the initiation into the early Church communities.

Some Christians understood that the Holy Spirit came as a part of baptism. Others did not. "'Did you receive the Holy Spirit when you became believers?' They answered him, 'we have never even heard that there is a Holy Spirit.' He said, 'How were you baptized?' They replied, 'With the baptism of John.' Paul then said, 'John baptized with a baptism of repentance, telling the people to believe in the one who was to come after him, that is, in Jesus.' When they heard this, they were baptized in the name of the Lord Jesus. And when Paul laid his hands on them, the Holy Spirit came upon them, and they spoke in tongues and prophesied." (Acts 19:2–6) The apostles also conferred the Holy Spirit through prayer and the laying on of hands, as well as anointing with oil.

From the third century onward, baptism and confirmation were celebrated just prior to the new Christians participating in their first eucharistic liturgy at the Easter Vigil. In the Middle Ages, anointing with oil became the primary symbol of the sacrament. Historical circumstances changed the way the sacrament was practiced. In 313, the Edict of Milan promulgated Christianity as legal in the Roman Empire. Because of the large number of converts, bishops in the Church found it difficult to get around to celebrate the baptisms. So, priests took over the baptisms, and the bishops were kept for the confirmation of the candidates.

In the last centuries of the first millennium, the churches of the East and West drifted apart. They became more distant from one another in terms of their ritual practice, theology, and church organization. Churches all over developed different sacramental practices.

Sacramental theology developed to the point that confirmation was recognized as a distinct sacrament by the late twelfth and early thirteenth centuries. Lombard (1095-1160) found confirmation to be the sacrament that bestowed the Holy Spirit. The Fourth Lateran Council (1215) distinguished it from the sacrament of baptism.

In the sixteenth century the Reformation happened. The sacraments became embroiled in controversy, and confirmation was labeled as nonsense because Martin Luther decided that there was no scriptural basis for the sacrament. Luther accepted only baptism and the Eucharist because he felt that the scriptural foundation for these sacraments was indisputable. Other Protestant reformers followed his example.

In response to the Reformation, the Council of Trent (1545-1563) clarified the Church's understanding of the sacraments and validated all seven sacraments as authentic. It also established the age of reason as the time when confirmation should be received.

Baptism, confirmation, and the Eucharist were connected as the sacraments of initiation with the Second Vatican Council. The Constitution on the Sacred Liturgy, written in 1963, decreed a reform of the rite of confirmation and the rite of baptism and highlighted them as a part of Christian initiation. RCIA (The Rite of Christian Initiation for Adults) was mandated for dioceses in the U.S. in 1988. This process has several stages within the full initiation: evangelization (precatechumenate), catechumenate, purification (enlightenment), and mystagogy.

The best way to understand the sacrament of confirmation is to see it as a part of the sacraments of initiation: baptism, confirmation, and the Eucharist. It is the one and same Holy Spirit that is celebrated at each of these three sacramental moments.

Some theologians emphasize that the sacraments of initiation should be celebrated together or as close together as possible. For others, confirmation is seen as a separate sacrament that ratifies or reaffirms baptism. In this view, confirmation is presently best celebrated with adolescents and young adults.

It is clear that the gift of the Holy Spirit is signified in both baptism and confirmation. The relation of these two sacraments to each other and to the overall process of Christian initiation is an issue that is still discussed today.

It was the practice of the Church to celebrate baptism and confirmation separately for many centuries. Confirmation lost much of the theological understanding of its character as a sacrament of initiation because of this separation. Instead, an additional bestowal of the Holy Spirit became identified with confirmation. Baptism was seen as a sacrament of initiation, while confirmation was associated with a strengthening of faith at a later stage in life. Confirmation was understood to empower people to make a public profession of faith and to strengthen them to defend the faith. With this thought, confirmation was a completion of baptism.

However, spiritual maturity is not necessarily connected to physical maturity. The Church did not require candidates to be adults. Children who had reached the age of reason could receive confirmation. The sacrament was not seen to be a rite of passage to Christian adulthood, which would result in an end to religious education. Instead the confirmed needed to take responsibility for furthering their own participation in the Church and its spiritual life.

The spirit is received only once by Christians in the New Testament. The spirit is received not by isolated individuals but in the context of the new Christian community. The spirit's role in the church community was a key element in the understanding of confirmation. In following the Second Vatican Council's mandate to reaffirm confirmation's original connections with Christian initiation, these passages about the early Church communities have to be taken into consideration.

When celebrated together as sacraments of initiation, the three sacraments work in harmony. The one to be baptized is brought into the life of Christ, then gifted with the Holy Spirit to be a true witness of Christ, and incorporated into the full eucharistic community. The spirit is not received in separate doses. Rather the spirit is at work throughout the initiation process by bringing the person to new life in Christ, within his or her community.

Confirmation is the means by which the Holy Spirit is poured out upon the baptized candidate, just as the Holy Spirit was given to the apostles at Pentecost. Anointing the individual on the forehead with chrism and the words, "Be sealed with the gift of the Holy Spirit," signifies the conferring of the Holy Spirit. The Holy Spirit draws the candidate closer to Christ. The Holy Spirit also strengthens the person to live as a witness of Christ.

Confirmation is a moment of grace that cannot be earned by displaying knowledge of our faith or by performing certain service tasks. Confirmation should acknowledge a deepening maturity in Christ and in the life of the Church. The entire parish community should welcome the spirit into their midst at the time of confirmation.

Confirmation is a sacrament of commitment in God's fidelity to us, and not just human commitment. At baptism, we hear the prayer that is said over the baptismal font: "Father, look now with love upon your Church, and unseal for her the fountain of baptism. By the power of the Holy Spirit give to the water of this font the grace of your Son. [Cleanse those to be baptized] from sin in a new birth of innocence by water and the Spirit."

In the rite of confirmation, we understand the implications of those baptismal words at the time when the bishop extends his hands over the candidates and prays: "All-powerful God, Father of our Lord Jesus Christ, by water and the Holy Spirit you freed your sons and daughters from sin and gave them new life. Send your Holy Spirit upon them to be their helper and guide. Give them the spirit of wisdom and understanding, the spirit of right judgment and courage, the spirit of knowledge and reverence. Fill them with the spirit of wonder and awe in your presence."

Earlier in the confirmation ceremony, the bishop asked the candidates to renew their baptismal promises, which their parents probably professed for them at the time of their infant baptism. The bishop went over each point of the creed that is said at the Sunday liturgy and had the young people respond to these statements:

At confirmation, we are anointed with the Holy Spirit. We ask the Spirit to impart each of the seven gifts of the Holy Spirit: wisdom, understanding, right judgment (counsel), courage (strength), knowledge, reverence (piety), and wonder (fear of the Lord).

Wisdom helps us recognize the importance of others and the importance of keeping God centered. This gift accounts for the soul's hunger for God and works in us along with the grace within us.

Understanding enables us to discover the meaning of our faith and to live according to its teachings. This gift helps us to know more clearly the mysteries of the faith.

Knowledge is the ability to think about and explore God's revelation and also to recognize there are mysteries of faith beyond us. Knowledge refers to learning the things we must do in order to do God's will.

Counsel is the ability to see the best way to follow God's plan when we have choices on how to live our faith.

Fortitude enables us to overcome obstacles to loving God and others, especially when it is difficult.

Piety helps us pray to God in true and loyal devotion. It helps us to honor and respect God and all people as children and images of God.

Fear of the Lord is the feeling of amazement before God, who is ever-present, and whose friendship we do not want to lose.

The origin of these seven gifts is found in Isaiah 11:1–3, where the qualities of the Messiah are foretold.

Catechetical Perspective

A bishop usually confers the sacrament of confirmation, although a delegate of the bishop may confer it as well. It is identified with the early teen years when the young people are facing serious moral and religious issues in their lives. The chrism oil used in the reception of the sacrament helps to strengthen the young person when facing difficult decisions in life.

Adults who have never received the sacrament should contact their pastor to see when they may be able to receive the sacrament. However, it is not necessary for a Catholic to be confirmed before being married in the Church.

Confirmation is a sacrament that is rich with ritual symbols. The following symbols help us to get the full meaning of the sacrament:

1. Baptism
Every confirmation begins with baptism, which is the first sacrament of initiation.

2. Community
The community is the sign of God's presence as you take another step in the initiation process.

3. Anointing
To the Jews, oil is the sign of God, and to Christians, Jesus was the anointed one. The Church has three holy oils. Holy chrism is the oil used in confirmation and holy orders. The other two oils are used in the anointing of the sick (oil of the sick) and in

baptism (oil of the catechumens). All of these oils are blessed by the bishop at the chrism Mass, which is held each year during the final week of Lent.

4. Touch

All seven sacraments have the symbol of touch. In confirmation, the bishop places his hand on the head of each one to be confirmed and prays that the Holy Spirit descends upon the one being confirmed.

5. Words

The words of the ceremony, the readings from Scripture, the words of the bishop at the time of the homily, the invitation of the presider for the call to be confirmed, as well as the prayer calling upon the Holy Spirit are all words that symbolize the meaning of the sacrament.

The words, "Be sealed with the gift of the Holy Spirit" preceded by your name is said at the time of the anointing. The candidate's baptismal name as well as his confirmation name is said, again tying the two sacraments together. The word "seal" draws upon historical times when a spot of hot wax was used to seal important documents. This distinctive seal was like the person's signature. In confirmation, God seals us as his anointed one permanently and eternally. This is the reason the sacrament of confirmation is only received once in a lifetime.

6. The bishop

The bishop or his delegate speaks on behalf of all of us, as he leads the prayer at the time of the sacrament. The bishop is also a symbol of the larger Church, which extends far beyond the immediate parish community.

7. The Eucharist

The Eucharist is the fulfillment and completion of the sacraments of initiation. The Eucharist is the repeatable part of the sacraments of initiation, as it is the one sacrament of the three initiation sacraments that can be received over and over. In each Eucharist the

Holy Spirit comes upon us again to renew and strengthen us for service in the Church.

In summarizing some of the basics of the sacrament, we find:

○ Confirmation is a sign of God's special love.
○ Confirmation is an invitation to deepen our relationship to God.
○ Confirmation includes a profession of faith by personally proclaiming our baptismal vows.
○ Confirmation is a lifelong challenge to live the way of Jesus.
○ Confirmation is a call to be a sign of God's presence.

Family Connection

○ **Take some time** to discuss the confirmation names of anyone in the family. Share why the names were chosen, if you know the reasons. If your family has a *Lives of the Saints* book, this is also a good time to talk about some of the saints, especially those who are less known.
○ **If your son or daughter** is receiving the sacrament of confirmation this year, encourage your friends and relatives to give the child a religious gift of some kind: a medal, a Bible, a book of prayers, a *Lives of the Saints* book, or a cross.
○ **The Holy Spirit** appeared to Jesus' disciples on the feast of Pentecost, which is considered the birthday of the Church. Use the feast of Pentecost to talk about how the Holy Spirit helps your family live as a Christian family.

CATECHETICAL ACTIVITY NO. 1

On a piece of 8 ½-by-11-inch paper, draw nine squares. Label each square with the following phrase:

My confirmation name is:_____

My confirmation sponsor was: _____

I was nervous about: _____

I am proud to be a Catholic because: _____

My service project was: _____

My best memory of confirmation was:_____

The bishop who confirmed me was: _____

I wanted to be confirmed because: _____

I was _____ years old when I got confirmed.

Ask each child to take the sheet home and ask an adult (parent, neighbor, teacher) to fill in each of the squares with an answer. Bring the sheet back to class and discuss the variety of answers.

CATECHETICAL ACTIVITY NO. 2

Write the seven gifts of the Holy Spirit on seven separate sheets of paper and put them into a basket or bowl. Divide the children into groups of two. Have each group draw a piece of paper from the basket or bowl. Give the children ten minutes to illustrate a particular gift of the Holy Spirit. Give each group time to perform its role-play for the entire class.

CATECHETICAL ACTIVITY NO. 3

In preparation for this activity, help the children know where to find stories about a variety of saints. Tell the children that they are to find a saint who lived with passion and love for God. If the children are younger, you may need to give examples of what passion and love for God would mean in everyday life. Places to find the stories could include *Lives of the Saints* books, the Internet (where stories about the saints could be found), or religion textbooks that the children have.

The coming of the Holy Spirit is often set in wind and fire. Give each child an 8 ½-by-11 sheet of red paper cut into the shape of a flame. On the flame, have each child write the name of a saint who lived with passion and love for God. Then have the child write several sentences on the flame telling what made him choose that particular saint. Share the stories of the saints with the entire class.

CATECHETICAL ACTIVITY NO. 4

Construct a confirmation wheel out of cardboard or wood to remind the children of the working of the Spirit in the lives of those being confirmed. The wheel would be similar to an Advent wreath. In the center of the wheel could be a white dove made of plastic or paper. The confirmation wheel has holes for seven red candles or it could have seven red votive candles. One candle is lit each week leading up to the celebration of the sacrament of confirmation. Next to each of the seven candles, write with a red marker the name of one of the gifts of the Holy Spirit. Each week as you light a candle, discuss with your class the meaning of that particular gift of the Spirit, and pray for those being confirmed in the upcoming weeks.

Concluding Remarks

Of the seven sacraments, confirmation is probably the sacrament most forgotten and least known. However, that could be because it revolves around the working of the Holy Spirit, who is often forgotten and the least known of the Trinity.

In the catechetical lesson about confirmation, emphasize the Holy Spirit as an advocate—someone who stands by a person's side and speaks up for him. The Holy Spirit will do that for the confirmed person. Just as the disciples changed after the coming of the Holy Spirit at Pentecost, so too, will the life of the confirmed person. Confirmation completes the grace of baptism and strengthens the confirmed person to use her gifts and talents to continue the work of Christ.

5

THE EUCHARIST

Rituals of age are very special. It is a momentous occasion when a child moves from a high chair to the table. The move brings new rules, manners, and conversation. The same is true when a child who has been baptized years before is finally able to join the adults at the table of the Eucharist. The child no longer needs the cry room or nursery at the parish church.

Some parishes have a Children's Liturgy of the Word (CLOW), which serves a wonderful purpose for those children who are ready for some catechesis during liturgy but who are unable to grasp the fullness of the liturgy by being able to understand the adult readings or being able to receive the Eucharist. This allows trained catechists to share the readings of the day in an age-appropriate way and prepare the children for that day when they will be ready to fully participate in the liturgy of the Eucharist.

Theology

The liturgical life of the Church revolves around the sacraments, with the Eucharist as the center.

If you were to ask ten people to describe what Eucharist means to them, you would get ten different answers.

○ For some, it is a meal.
○ For others, it is a memorial of Christ's sacrifice.
○ For some, it is a community gathering.

- For others, it is a personal prayer.
- For some, it is a sacred ritual.
- For others, it is a celebration of the Last Supper.
- For some, it is a remembrance what has happened in the past.
- For others, it is a celebration of something in the present.
- For some, it is called the Mass.
- For others, it is called the Eucharist.

Who's right and who's wrong? In essence all of the above facets are right. The Eucharist is all of these things and more. No matter how many courses one takes and homilies one hears on the topic of the Eucharist, there always seems to be a new aspect.

Some early communities connected the celebration with the reenactment of the Last Supper and did not celebrate often. Some other early communities celebrated often because they looked at the Eucharist as daily food and sustenance for life.

If we look at the history of the Eucharist, we find that initially it was referred to as the breaking of bread since it was at a Jewish meal when Jesus broke the bread and drank the wine and changed it to his Body and Blood. In a similar manner, the early Jewish followers gathered to break the bread and share it with one another. The word "Eucharist" means "thanksgiving," and Christians gather to give thanks to God for the gift of Jesus himself.

The Lord's Supper, where Jesus gathered and first changed the bread and wine to his Body and Blood, is linked to Calvary, where he sacrificed himself for us. We call the Eucharist "liturgy" because God's works are celebrated publicly. We call the Eucharist "worship" because we bow down before the Lord, thanking him for his sacrifice. We call the Eucharist "the Mass" because it concludes with sending forth the congregation into the world to witness to the greatness of God. We call the Eucharist "sacrifice" because the meaning and effects of Jesus' death on Calvary are encountered each time we celebrate the Eucharist. Christians would speak of the sacrifice of the Mass because they believed that we partake in the fruits of Jesus' death each time we share his Body and Blood.

The Mass is also a meal because its roots are traced back to the Last Supper on Holy Thursday, when Jesus shared a meal with his disciples. At that meal Jesus told the disciples to share bread and wine in his memory. Just as the Last Supper led to Calvary, so, too, must the Eucharist lead us to commitment and sacrifice in our daily lives.

The Second Vatican Council spoke of the fourfold presence of Jesus in the Mass. Jesus is present in the assembly, in the word, in the ministers and under the appearance of bread and wine. We will look at each of these four aspects separately.

We think of ourselves as the assembly of God, God's own people. The group of disciples who dispersed on Good Friday and who came back strengthened by the Spirit after the resurrection of Jesus became a community of believers and referred to themselves as the assembly of God.

Catholics are rediscovering the treasures and power of the Scriptures, the word of God. It is in the proclamation of the Scriptures at Mass that Jesus' presence should be most clearly expressed. The homily interprets the Scriptures, and then the assembly responds with the profession of faith. Personal prayer, reflection and study of Scriptures should continue to be a part of the ongoing formation of each person.

The ordained priest has a crucial role in the celebration of the Mass, as he presides over the assembly. The priest interprets the Scriptures in the homily and changes the bread and wine into the Body and Blood of Christ. Christ is present to the community of believers in the ordained priest, as well as in the ministers of Communion, the cantors and the lectors.

We encounter the peak of Jesus' presence at the Mass in the appearance of bread and wine. The bread and wine become the Body and Blood of Christ through the words of the priest and the action of the Holy Spirit. This is a core belief for us as Catholics. The ultimate act of faith for a Catholic is to receive the bread and wine at Mass and know that it is truly the Body and Blood of Christ.

The Eucharist is the sacramental action of giving thanks and praise to the Father. It is the sacrificial memorial of Christ and his body, the Church, and is the continuing presence of Christ in his word and in his Spirit. The bread and wine become Christ himself. *(GDC)*

Catechetical Perspective

Children's preparation for the Eucharist begins in the home. The family has a most important role in communicating the essence of the eucharistic celebration in the parish. Reflect on the many meals that you have shared around the table. Think of the ordinary daily breakfast, in which you may be rushed to eat and get off to work or to school. The dinner may be more relaxed, giving you time to discuss the happenings of the day. Think of times when perhaps you had a dinner guest who had come to your home for encouragement or comfort. This is a time when your child listens to what you say, absorbs your values and looks to you for direction.

There was a long list under the Theology section of possible ways in which we as Catholics believe in the Eucharist. Which of those facets do you emphasize at a time of the family meal? Or should you include a combination such as community gathering, personal prayer, and ritual? As a catechist, it is important for you to build upon this home experience, while still being sensitive to the variety of home situations.

The official Church documents call the Mass the source and

summit of the Christian life. We know that in the early Church the people gathered to break bread and to remember what Jesus did and said and what Jesus told them to do in his memory.

After Jesus' resurrection we know that he often appeared at mealtime to his followers. The Eucharist is very important because it is the primary way in which Catholics connect with Jesus and his breaking of the bread. The Eucharist is the sacrament from which all of the other six sacraments draw their meaning.

One of the most popular stories of Jesus after his resurrection is his appearance to his disciples on the road to Emmaus. "It was a few days after Jesus died on the cross. Two of the disciples were going to a town called Emmaus. They talked about Jesus as they walked along the road. Jesus came near the disciples. He began to talk with them. The disciples did not know that Jesus had been raised from the dead. They did not recognize him. They arrived in Emmaus and the disciples invited Jesus to stay with them. They sat down to eat. Then Jesus took the bread in his hands. He blessed the bread. He broke it and gave it to the disciples. Then they knew he was Jesus. They recognized Jesus when he broke the bread." (From Luke 24:13–35).

The center of the life of the Church is celebrating the Eucharist. Several guidelines about the Eucharist would be important to review with the children in your class, especially if they have previously received their first Eucharist.

○ One must be a baptized Catholic to receive the Eucharist, which is truly the Body and Blood of Jesus.
○ One should fast one hour before receiving Eucharist, including any food or drink except for water and for what is needed to take with medicine.
○ It is encouraged that Catholics receive Communion each time they go to Mass. Catholics must receive Communion at least

once a year during the Easter season, which lasts from the first Sunday of Lent to Trinity Sunday.

○ Catholics may not receive Communion if they have committed a mortal sin and have not yet gone to the sacrament of reconciliation.

○ Venial sins are forgiven by receiving the Eucharist.

○ Communion may be received either in the hand or on the tongue.

○ Some parishes offer Communion under both species of bread and wine. It is the decision of the individual as to whether or not to receive both the bread and wine. No matter what decision is made, one still receives the Body and Blood of Christ.

As a catechist, focus on the fact that the Catholic Church teaches Jesus' real presence in the Eucharist and that the unleavened bread and wine are not just blessed symbols, but they become the Body and Blood of Jesus by the power of the Holy Spirit. Jesus is truly present.

Family Connection

○ **It is important** to celebrate the Eucharist together as a family, whenever possible. Volunteer to bring up the gifts as a part of the offertory procession.

○ **The Last Supper** is the meal Jesus celebrated when he instituted the Eucharist. Bread and wine became the Body and Blood of Christ. After talking about the story of the Last Supper, give your child (or children) a piece of unlined paper, a ruler, a pencil and a quarter. Ask your child to draw a picture of the Last Supper using only geometric shapes, such as circles, rectangles, triangles, etc. Use the pencil and ruler to draw lines, and use the quarter (or get a penny) for the circles. After drawing the Last Supper, have your child color the Last Supper using markers. If you want, you could take your child's picture and transfer it to a T-shirt or hang the picture on the refrigerator.

○ **In the story of Jesus** sharing bread and wine with his apostles on the road to Emmaus, the disciples recognized Jesus because of breaking the bread and drinking the wine. At Mass, we receive the gift of Jesus himself. We share ourselves with Jesus as we are peacemakers. Discuss with your family how to be peacemakers with family and with neighbors. Share a sign of peace with your family.

○ **At the Last Supper**, Jesus left his Body and Blood in the Eucharist to his disciples so that they would not forget how much he loved them. With your family, talk about what you would leave each other if you were going away and wanted to remind each other how much you loved them. Read the story of the Last Supper (Luke 22:14–20) after the discussion.

○ **If your child** is going to be receiving the sacrament of the Eucharist for the first time this year, be sure to participate in all of the offerings from your local parish in preparation. These could include a family retreat or day of reflection on the sacrament. Also, there will probably be sessions held from the catechetical leader to share the specifics of the actual eucharistic celebrations.

CATECHETICAL ACTIVITY NO. 1

Go to the grocery store and buy the frozen bread that is in the shape of rolls.

Put one roll for each child on a cookie sheet to thaw.

While the roll is thawing, go to your computer and type a Scripture passage that has to do with the Eucharist. Usually you can find an age-appropriate passage in the child's religion textbook on the chapter about the Eucharist or pick a passage of your own choosing. One option for this Scripture passage is, "This is my body which will be given for you; do this in memory of me…This cup is the new covenant in my blood, which will be shed for you." (Luke 22:19–20)

Make enough copies of the passage for each child. Take the copy and stuff the small piece of paper into the thawed dough.

Let the dough continue to rise until the piece of paper can no longer be seen.

Bake the rolls in your oven, following the directions on the grocery package.

When the rolls are finished baking, put the rolls in a wicker basket and take them to your catechetical session. Use as a part of a prayer service.

Play the first verse of a song using a CD that has the theme of the Eucharist.

Give each child a baked roll, and ask each child to "break open the word" by reading the passage.

Play another verse of the song while the children are eating the roll. You may want to take some grape juice to serve with the roll.

CATECHETICAL ACTIVITY NO. 2

Invite your local pastor to talk about what the Eucharist means to him as a priest. Prepare any questions in advance for the priest. Don't let the talk go very long. Remember the rules for a good speaker: "Be brief. Be bright. Be gone."

CATECHETICAL ACTIVITY NO. 3

Make a set of flashcards for each child in your class. Have the child review the flashcards at home, and then have them use them in class, matching the flashcard of the word with the flashcard of the definition. Here are some examples of the flashcards and definitions:

ALTAR—The table where the Eucharist is celebrated in church.
ASSEMBLY—The people who gather for the liturgy.
BAPTISM—The sacrament that the person needs to receive before receiving Eucharist.

CHALICE—The special cup used at the liturgy of the Eucharist to hold the wine that becomes the Blood of Christ.

CONSECRATION—The rite of the Mass where the bread and wine become the Body and Blood of Christ.

EUCHARIST—The word means "give thanks" and is the sacrament of the real presence of Jesus under the appearances of bread and wine.

HOLY COMMUNION—Receiving the Body and Blood of Jesus.

HOST—The name for the bread we use at Mass.

LORD'S SUPPER—Another name for the Eucharist.

MASS—Has two main parts: Liturgy of the Word and Liturgy of the Eucharist.

SACRAMENTS OF INITIATION—Baptism, confirmation, and Eucharist.

TABERNACLE—A special place where the blessed sacrament is reserved in church.

CATECHETICAL ACTIVITY NO. 4

Construct or design an altar. The altar is the church's dinner table. The altar is one of the most important pieces of furniture in the church, as it is on the altar that the bread and wine is changed into the Body and Blood of Christ. When you have the children construct or design an altar, ask them why they chose the shape that they did. For example, did some of them make their altars in a circle, or were they all rectangular since that is what they see in church? What material would they use to construct their altar? Wood? Stone? Metal? Why? What does the designed altar say about Jesus' presence in the Eucharist?

CATECHETICAL ACTIVITY NO. 5

Jesus is the Bread of Life. In the Eucharist we are fed with the Bread of Life. If there is consecrated bread left over after Communion during Mass, it is put in the tabernacle and is called the "Blessed Sacrament." This consecrated bread is used to take Communion to the sick and at the time of a Communion service in church. This consecrated bread is also used during the Good Friday service, since there is no Mass on that day.

Bring to your class examples of breads from other cultures and nationalities, depending upon what you can find at your local stores. Talk to the class about bread being an important part of life and often one of the most important foods within a culture. After the discussion, share the various breads by tearing pieces from the various breads. Savor the texture, the smell, and the taste of each kind of bread. Notice how satisfying a taste of bread can be. Compare this to the nourishment one gets at the Eucharist. Just as daily bread satisfies our physical hunger, so too, does the Eucharist satisfy our spiritual hunger.

CATECHETICAL ACTIVITY NO. 6

The Emmaus story (Luke 24:13–35) is one of the most important Eucharist stories in the Gospel. Have the children role-play the story by adding actions while you read the story aloud.

Concluding Remarks

Just as confirmation was once one of the least-known sacraments, the Eucharist is one of the most well-known sacraments. From the time of baptism, a first communicant has been one with Jesus. Taking a place at the table of the Lord marks a new stage in one's relationship with Christ. There is a conscious willingness to let the Lord nourish and nurture what began at baptism.

In the catechetical setting, each person is a part of the nurturing that began at baptism. A child may not understand the full implications and meaning of turning one's life over to the Lord. And possibly, neither does the adult catechist. Few can boast of genuine holiness. That is why each Catholic keeps coming to the Lord's table for nourishment. That is the message of the catechist: this is a work in progress. This will only come to completion when one partakes of the heavenly feast that is being prepared for those who love the Lord.

6

RECONCILIATION

A mother and her children were killed in an automobile accident. They were leaving the mother's parents' home early on Sunday morning, after celebrating a birthday the previous evening. A young man who had been out all night had fallen asleep in his car, sideswiping the family car, which held all six family members. The father and two other children survived the accident.

Under very difficult circumstances, the father did a great job rearing the two children, staying in close touch with the mother's family instead of distancing himself, as he could have.

Any time we hear the horrific details of this or any other accident, people wonder if it is possible to forgive the person who caused the accident. Holding a grudge is one of the biggest obstacles to complete forgiveness. Family members needed to let go and put the deep hurt behind them. Only then was the healing power of forgiveness unleashed.

Theology

The sacrament of reconciliation was previously called the sacrament of penance, and words such as confession and confessional were commonly used. Confession names only one part of the sacrament, while reconciliation names what is most important about the sacrament: the forgiveness of our sins by God. Reconciliation brings the richness of the peace that comes when there is no longer friction or discord. Reconciliation brings us into harmony with God and with one another. It is God's mercy that heals us as sinners and calls us to a conversion of heart.

Forgiveness is rooted in the Gospel passage: "On the evening of his resurrection, Jesus sent his apostles out to reconcile sinners to his Father and commissioned them to forgive sins in his name: 'Peace be with you. As the Father has sent me, so I send you.' And when he had said this, he breathed on them and said to them, 'Receive the Holy Spirit. Whose sins you forgive are forgiven them, and whose sins you retain are retained.'" (John 20:21–23)

Forgiveness is a part of each of our lives, sometimes in momentous ways such as the experience that I had in my sister's death, and other times, in very small ways. A vital part of our faith is learning how to forgive. When we choose to act selfishly by putting ourselves before God and others, we sin. A sin is a free decision to do what we know is wrong or to fail to do what we know is right.

Young children, in particular, can be confused by the difference between a mistake or accident and a sin. It is important that the children are clear on this. Giving example after example is usually one of the better ways to teach this concept. This would be done before moving on to the specifics of the types of sin.

Mortal sin is a serious offense against God and the Christian community. Three conditions make a sin mortal: The act must be seriously wrong, we must know that the act is seriously wrong, and we still freely choose to do the wrong. The Church teaches that "individual, integral confession and absolution remain the only ordinary way for the faithful to reconcile themselves with God and Church, unless physical or moral impossibility excuses from this kind of confession. The faithful are obliged to confess all serious sins." *(Code of Canon Law)*

A venial sin is a less serious offense. Our relationship with God is weakened by venial sins, but our relationship with God and the community is not destroyed.

There are three different forms of the sacrament of reconciliation: The Rite for the Reconciliation of Individual Penitents; the Rite for the Reconciliation of Several Penitents; and the Rite for the Reconciliation of Several Penitents with General Absolution. The first one of these is the usual form when a penitent goes to church, and goes into the reconciliation room and celebrates the sacrament with an individual priest. In the reconciliation room, there is usually the choice of face-to-face or behind a screen for anonymity.

The second rite is exemplified when a parish holds a penance service and invites numerous priests to facilitate the number of people attending the service. There is usually a communal preparation first with songs, readings, and perhaps a homily. Then the individual penitents meet with an individual priest to confess their sins and receive absolution. Our sins are personal but never private. There is no sin that does not have repercussions on the entire church community and the human family. Therefore the communal rite is most appropriate and has taken on some popularity in Catholic parishes.

The third rite is used only in exceptional situations, such as a major accident. The penitent does not mention individual sins to a priest. There is a single, general absolution to all those gathered for the sacrament. However, if someone has committed a mortal sin, he must still receive individual absolution at a later time. If he does not receive individual absolution later, he worsens the mortal sin.

People's need for the sacrament of reconciliation is in proportion to their holiness, not their sinfulness. Therefore you will hear great saints talk about being great sinners. They understand more than most of us what is involved in loving God and staying true to God's laws of love.

Catechetical Perspective

Preparing children for the sacrament of reconciliation poses unique challenges. Children are very perceptive when it comes to detecting the sincerity of adults. There was a time when frequent confession (once a week or at least once a month) was part of the normal mode of operation for a Catholic. In Catholic schools, the children were marched over to church to go to confession prior to each and every first Friday. There used to be long lines of penitents on Saturday afternoon. This is no longer the case. Therefore when an adult tries to explain to the child the importance of receiving the sacrament often, sincerity comes into question. How can we convincingly communicate that this sacrament is a vital piece in the spiritual development of a person, when the child does not see the adult celebrating the sacrament? This is one of the challenges.

Children need a lot of reassurance about making their first confession and about continuing to celebrate the sacrament on a regular basis. A child needs to be assured that God does not measure whether or not to forgive us by how well we forgive others. We stress to the children that we celebrate God's forgiveness when we receive the sacrament of reconciliation. The idea of Catholic guilt has been around for many years, and it is important that we do not instill in a child this guilt complex. This is another challenge.

God's unconditional love and forgiveness should be front and center in the catechesis of reconciliation. What is most important in this sacrament is what God does. Our examination of conscience as well as the confession of our sins is much less important than the forgiveness of our sins. "Go in peace. Your sins are forgiven." This is truly the greatest gift of the sacrament of reconciliation.

The best way to tell the children about God's unconditional love and forgiveness is to show how Jesus lived this while on earth. Several Scripture passages particularly help the children to see this.

The story of the Good Shepherd (Luke 15:4–5) inspires in children a genuine hope and belief in a loving and caring God. The shepherd cared for one hundred sheep, but there were only ninety-nine when the shepherd counted them. One sheep was gone. The shepherd went out immediately to look for the lost sheep, instead of waiting for the sheep to come home on its own. The shepherd stayed out until he found the lost sheep. Like the shepherd in the story, Jesus never leaves us alone or lost, even if we have sinned.

The story of the Prodigal Son (Luke 15: 11–24) is more about the forgiveness and love of the father than the repentance of the son. The son left the father's home with his inheritance and went far away. He squandered everything his father had given to him. Then he decided to go home to his father, and beg for forgiveness and mercy. The father not only forgave him, but also showed him his greatest generosity. This far exceeded any expectation. In fact, the original audience hearing Jesus' story would have been shocked by the details of the story. Would anyone have the courage to ask for his inheritance at such a young age? Would a Jewish boy feed pigs? Would the father have given such a son a ring that in essence bestowed authority and power over the finances of the family?

The details of this story show that the father was highly unusual, just as God is highly unusual for forgiving us no matter what.

Some other Scripture choices to use with the children are:

Mark 2:1–12	Jesus heals a paralyzed man
Mark 2:13–17	Jesus eats with sinners and tax collectors
Luke 15:8–10	The parable of the Lost Coin
Luke 19:1–10	Jesus forgives Zaccheus

Children learn developmentally. What is considered adequate teaching to a second-grader on topics such as grace, sin, forgiveness, and the Ten Commandments isn't adequate for a fourth-, sixth- or eighth-grader. Therefore it is critical that these topics continue to be revisited. The *NDC* calls for continuing formation beyond the child's first reconciliation: "Since conversion is a lifelong process, catechesis for the sacrament of penance and reconciliation is ongoing. Children have a right to a fuller catechesis each year." (*NDC* 36B-2 or *NDC* 126)

This ongoing catechesis can take place by holding a series of classes on the theme of forgiveness and reconciliation each year, as a part of the catechetical program. Advent and Lent are two common times for these classes, as the parishes often have a communal celebration of the sacrament during these special times of the year. Check your textbook, and see if there are classes on the sacrament of reconciliation already planned as a part of the year. If not, use the information in this book or in some other book that you can find, in order to help you with some catechesis and activities on the topic.

Family Connection

❍ **Celebrate the sacrament of reconciliation** as a family. At some time during Advent and Lent each parish usually holds a reconciliation service for the entire parish. Make plans to attend as a family.

❍ **Take turns at the dinner table** sharing stories of when you have forgiven each other or others.

❍ **Put a lighted candle** on the dinner table, talking to your child about the need to be a "light of the world" by sharing forgiveness and showing kindness to others.

CATECHETICAL ACTIVITY NO. 1

As a tool for examining one's conscience, we will look at some traits of animals—traits that are OK for an animal, but not OK when we act that way.

THE DONKEY—Donkeys are single-minded and often do not go where their owners want them to go.

How often have you been stubborn and not done what your parents wanted you to do?

Have you been asked to help someone and found an excuse not to help?

THE ELEPHANT—Elephants have thick skin; but they also have a long memory. If a trainer mistreats an elephant, he does not cooperate the next time.

How often have you refused to give someone another chance? Do you cooperate with your parents and your teachers, even if they are having a bad day, and may have "mistreated" you?

THE LION—The lion is considered the "king of the jungle." He attacks weaker animals and acts like a bully.

How often have you bullied a classmate? When have you picked on someone who was less popular than you? Have you helped someone who is being bullied by others?

After studying these examples, have the children come up with examples of their own. Put the entire list together in forming an examination of conscience. As a catechist, have some examples prepared that cover each of the commandments.

CATECHETICAL ACTIVITY NO. 2

This activity can be used as an example of encouraging an attitude of tolerance and forgiveness:

Go to the store and buy a jar or bag of colored popcorn. If you are not familiar with colored popcorn, look on the shelf in the grocery store with the regular popcorn, not microwave popcorn.

You will also need a way to pop the popcorn in class. As a recommendation, a hot-air popcorn popper works great to use in a classroom, as all you need is a power outlet, no stove top or microwave.

Take the colored popcorn to your class and give each child several kernels of varied colors. Ask questions such as:

How are the popcorn kernels different? Different size? Different shape? Different colors?

How are the popcorn kernels alike? Similar size? Similar shape? Similar colors?

How are the children here in the class different? Different color hair? Different color eyes? Different heights?

How are the children in the class alike? Similar age? Similar location where they live? Similar school that they attend?

Note: You can enhance these questions as much as you would like, depending upon the age of children in your class.

Then take one-half cup of colored popcorn and put it in the hot-air popcorn popper. When it pops, all the colored kernels will pop white. The children (of any age) will find this fascinating!

Talk about how even though the kernels looked different, they now look alike.

Talk about how even though the children look different, there are many similarities. Talk about how we need to be tolerant and accept children who may be different from us.

Close the activity by reading 1 Corinthians 12:12–14:

"As a body is one though it has many parts, and all the parts of the body, though many, are one body, so also Christ. For in one Spirit we were all baptized into one body....now the body is not a single part, but many.

If you are working with children over the age of ten, you may want to use the full reading of 1 Corinthians 12:12–26.

CATECHETICAL ACTIVITY NO. 2B

If you're unable to have a popcorn popper in the classroom, you could use this activity for children of any age, looking at the virtue of tolerance and acceptance of others. In this case the milk and food colors swirl and mix, showing that although we started as very separate entities, Jesus and the Church can bring us together as one.

SUPPLIES: one-quarter cup whole milk, one teaspoon liquid dish-washing detergent, four wooden toothpicks, one small container that has been thoroughly washed and dried, four different colors of liquid food coloring.

DIRECTIONS

1. Pour about one-quarter cup of whole milk into the container. This should be about one-half-inch deep.
2. Place a drop of each of four different food colors on the milk in the container, in opposite corners from one another.
3. Dip a toothpick into liquid dish-washing detergent, then touch the toothpick into the middle of the dish. What happens?
4. Try again with more detergent, touching the milk in different areas.

CATECHETICAL ACTIVITY NO. 3

After reviewing the rite of reconciliation, get a large roll of shelf paper or poster boards. Have the children draw the "steps" for celebrating the sacrament of reconciliation:

- ○ Introductory rite—a song and prayer by the priest
- ○ The word of God—readings and homily
- ○ Examination of conscience—think of ways we have sinned
- ○ Rite of reconciliation
- ○ Individual welcome by the priest
- ○ Confession of sins and priest gives a penance
- ○ Act of contrition
- ○ Absolution
- ○ Prayer of thanksgiving
- ○ Concluding prayer or song by entire group

The visual depiction will help to instill the "routine" into their minds.

CATECHETICAL ACTIVITY NO. 4

Take a Scripture story that has a theme of reconciliation and tell the story to the class. If you have a children's Bible, this could be a good age-appropriate tool to use for telling the story. As you tell the story, pause after each sentence and have the children respond with the "emotion" connected to the sentence: "yeah, oh no," or "gasp." Practice each of the three emotions with the children, in advance of telling the story. Here is how it would work, using the story of the Good Samaritan (based on Luke 10:29–37).

Catechist: Jesus told a story of a man who was traveling on a road, when robbers attacked a man on the road.

Children: Oh no!

Catechist:	The robbers hurt the man.
Children:	Oh no!
Catechist:	The robbers stole everything the man had.
Children:	Oh no!
Catechist:	Running away, they left the man lying on the ground.
Children:	Oh no!
Catechist:	A traveler soon came down the road.
Children:	Yeah!
Catechist:	He saw the injured man lying on the road.
Children:	Yeah!
Catechist:	But he chose to walk by without helping him.
Children:	Oh no!
Catechist:	A second traveler came down the road.
Children:	Yeah!
Catechist:	But he also chose to walk by without helping him.
Children:	Oh no!
Catechist:	Then a traveler from Samaria came down the road.
Children:	Gasp!
Catechist:	This traveler stopped.
Children:	Gasp!
Catechist:	This traveler bandaged the man's wounds.
Children:	Yeah!
Catechist:	He put the man on his donkey and brought the injured man to an inn.
Children:	Yeah!
Catechist:	He paid the innkeeper to take care of the injured man, expecting nothing in return.
Children:	Yeah!

Discuss with the children times when they have seen someone be a Good Samaritan. Discuss with the children times when they could have responded differently in a situation, and could have instead been a Good Samaritan.

CATECHETICAL ACTIVITY NO. 5

Get a set of plastic knives and forks commonly used at picnics. On the set of knives, use a permanent marking pen to write numerals one through ten. On the set of forks, use the marking pen to write two or three words that describe each commandment. Distribute the ten numbered knives to the children, and distribute the ten commandment forks to other children. Then give the children time to find their matching partner. For example, the child with the No. 4 knife will find the fork that says, "honor parents." Continue until each child has matched the commandment number with the description.

Concluding Remarks

Through the sacrament of reconciliation, the person receives God's forgiveness. Forgiveness requires being sorry for sins committed, as well as the resolve not to sin again. Forgiveness is a part of everyday life; therefore this sacrament is most understood by children.

Remind the children that how they live each day is the basis of their relationship with God. Each person has at some time inadvertently "messed up" when it comes to following the Lord perfectly. Luckily Jesus isn't waiting to pounce on anyone and condemn them for every misdemeanor. It is a lifelong journey to purify the mind and heart.

7

ANOINTING OF THE SICK

S ome people are blessed with longevity of life, while others struggle with health issues from the time they are children. Some elderly people volunteer at a local nursing home and do other volunteer work "where those old people need help." Their motto in life is to take "one day at a time." They want more hours to accomplish all that they believe they were put on earth to accomplish. They have a love of people and of life that is quite extraordinary. In contrast, other older people complain that the days drag on and they wish the days would go by faster.

One aspect of the Catholic faith that has a significant meaning to older people is the sacrament of the anointing of the sick. They want to be prepared whenever God calls them home to heaven. Besides the regular celebration of the sacrament of reconciliation, many also participate in the anointing of the sick whenever it is offered at the local parish. Elderly people who are ill or in the hospital should ask that a priest come and celebrate the sacrament of the anointing of the sick with them. This is a true understanding of the grace of a sacrament that Catholics often overlook.

Theology

In the Old Testament, sickness was seen as a sign of weakness and somehow bound up with sin. The prophets wanted people to believe that sickness could serve as redemption for both one's own sins, as well as the sins of others. "Because of his affliction he shall see the light in fullness of days; through his suffering, my servant shall justify many, and their guilt he shall bear." (Isaiah 53:11) In an earlier passage, Isaiah also tells of God forgiving their guilt and healing their sickness. Illness becomes a way to conversion.

Christ's compassion toward the sick is documented in Scripture. It is easy to find numerous stories where Jesus has healed someone. The Gospel of Mark, in particular, is filled with people who try to touch Jesus to be healed, and where Jesus lays on his hands to heal. Jesus uses everyday items such as mud and his hands in order to heal. By Jesus' own passion and death, he gave new meaning to our suffering. It can be a means of purification and salvation, as well as a victory over sin, suffering, and death. Jesus makes the miseries his own. Jesus "took away our infirmities and bore our diseases." (Matthew 8:17) Similarly, in the sacrament of the anointing of the sick, Jesus continues to touch in order to heal.

"This sacred anointing of the sick was instituted by Christ our Lord as a true and proper sacrament of the New Testament. It is alluded to indeed by Mark, but is recommended to the faithful and promulgated by James the apostle." (*CCC* 1511). The chief biblical text concerning the rite is James 5:14–15. "Is any among you sick? Let him call for the elders of the church, and let them pray over him, anointing him with oil in the name of the Lord; and the prayer of faith will save the sick man, and the Lord will raise him up; and if he has committed sins, he will be forgiven."

For many years, this sacrament was called "Extreme Unction" based on the fact that it was given most exclusively to those who were at the point of death.

According to the Second Vatican Council, the sacrament is to be given to those who are ill or aged, as well as those on death's door. "The anointing of the sick is not a sacrament for those only who are at the point of death. Hence, as soon as anyone of the faithful begins to be in danger of death from sickness or old age, the fitting time for him to receive this sacrament has certainly arrived." (*CCC* 1514)

One change that has taken place over the years with this sacrament is that it is now regularly celebrated as a communal celebration. The sacrament can be received in the context of liturgy, at a special service, or at the individual's home or hospital bed. Only priests are ministers of the sacrament.

Contrary to sacraments such as baptism and confirmation, this sacrament may be received more than once. When a sick person recovers from the illness, he may receive the sacrament when he becomes ill again later. An elderly person may receive the sacrament as he becomes frail over the years.

The sacrament confers a special grace, which unites the sick or elderly person with the passion of Christ. It gives comfort, peace, courage and the forgiveness of sins if the sick or elderly person is not able to make an individual confession.

Catechetical Perspective

When teaching children a lesson on the sacrament of the anointing of the sick, it is often more difficult because sickness and death seem far away. Yet, as you would brainstorm about their experiences with sick or older people, each child probably knows someone who is in need of the graces of the sacrament.

Any member of the church can receive this sacrament, regardless of age. Therefore if you are at a community celebration of the sacrament of the anointing of the sick, it is not unusual to see young and middle-aged people there as well as the elderly. The sacrament is for those who are sick or who are of old age. It is important to remember that sickness can involve more than bodily illness.

Mental and spiritual problems can affect our physical health. A new mother may be suffering from postpartum depression. Unemployment can cause depression or ulcers. Persons suffering from addictions can be anointed. In these cases the person does not have to be hospitalized or institutionalized in order to celebrate the sacrament. The comfort and healing touch of Jesus is at the center of this sacrament. The parish community needs to see the faith of the people coming to receive this sacrament. The recipients are putting their faith in God. It is an act of faith. The celebration of the sacrament should be preceded by individual confession, if possible.

If the sacrament is being celebrated in a hospital or in a home, the celebration of the sacrament is essentially the anointing with oil on the forehead and hands of the sick or elderly person. This anointing with oil is accompanied by the prayer of the priest who asks for special blessing and grace upon the person receiving the sacrament. "[S]end the power of your Holy Spirit, the Consoler, into this precious oil...Make this oil a remedy for all who are anointed with it; heal them in body, in soul and in spirit, and deliver them from every affliction." *(Pastoral Care of the Sick* No. 123) The priest invites all who are present to join in the Lord's Prayer. Communion may be received at this time, and a blessing for all present is given.

If the sacrament is being celebrated as a communal celebration at liturgy, then the anointing is usually done after the homily. A litany of prayers is said for those who will be anointed and for those who care for them. The sick are invited to come forward to the altar. There the priest lays his hands on the head of the person to be anointed, recalling Jesus' way of healing: "At sunset, all who had people sick with various diseases brought them to him. He laid his hands on them on each of them and cured them." (Luke 4:40)

Blessed oil is brought to the altar. A prayer is said over the oil. The priest then makes a sign of the cross with the oil on the sick person's forehead, saying: "Through this holy anointing may the Lord in his love and mercy help you with the grace of the Holy

Spirit." All respond "Amen." Then the priest anoints the palms of the sick one's hands with the sign of the cross: "May the Lord who frees you from sin save you and raise you up." All respond "Amen." The liturgy then continues with the bread and wine being brought to the altar for the offertory.

As you catechize children about this sacrament, it is important to remind children that healing always takes place as a result of this sacrament; however, the healing may not be of the physical nature. We believe in prayer that God answers our prayers. Sometimes the answer is "no" or "not yet" instead of the "yes" that we wanted. In this sacrament we pray that the sick be healed in body, in soul and in spirit. So while we do not see physical healing, that does not mean that no healing has taken place.

The special grace of the sacrament of the anointing of the sick has as its effects:

○ the uniting of the sick person to the passion of Christ, for his own good and that of the whole Church;
○ the strengthening, peace, and courage to endure in a Christian manner the sufferings of illness or old age;
○ the forgiveness of sins, if the sick person was not able to obtain it through the sacrament of Penance;
○ the restoration of health, if it is conducive to the salvation of his soul;
○ the preparation for passing over to eternal life. (*CCC* 1532)

Family Connection

○ **As a family,** visit one of your elderly relatives or a neighbor once a week or once a month, as time allows.

○ **Invite the elderly relative or neighbor** to share a meal with your family.

○ **Have one of your older children** help to do chores for an elderly relative or neighbor, at no charge to the person.

○ **Visit someone in the hospital** or nursing home. Make a card for the person or bring something for the person to keep in her room as a reminder of the love of God.

○ **Purchase Christmas cards** or other greeting cards that support the efforts of Saint Jude's Children's Hospital or some other charity that supports sick children.

○ **Have a sick-call set** in your home; never be without blessed candles. This set can be ordered online or bought at a Catholic religious goods store. Cultivate the correct attitude within your family in regard to this sacrament; don't fear it.

○ **Assist sick neighbors** in getting a priest to their home.

CATECHETICAL ACTIVITY NO. 1

As a class, make greeting cards for those in hospitals and nursing homes. For young children, let them design their own cards. If possible, it is nice to have a small group deliver the cards to the nursing home.

CATECHETICAL ACTIVITY NO. 2

For older children, give each student a Bible, and have them find the Book of Psalms. Tell them: Imagine that you work for a greeting card designer. Your job is to design get-well and sympathy cards using a passage from the Psalms. For example, Psalm 61:2–3, "Hear O God, my cry; listen to my prayer. From the earth's end,

I call to you as my heart grows faint" could be used as the inside verse in a get-well card. The newly designed cards could be given out in hospitals or nursing homes. The sympathy cards could be sent to families in the parish who have recently lost a loved one.

CATECHETICAL ACTIVITY NO. 3

Hold a "games" afternoon on a Saturday or Sunday for the elderly. Bingo, Farkle, Dominoes, and Yahtzee are a few games that the elderly would know how to play. Serve simple refreshments after the games.

Concluding Remarks

God is always ready to help those in need. There are probably few groups that are more in need than the sick or elderly. This is the sacrament just for them. God wants to reach out his healing hand to those persons.

For children, being elderly seems very far away. Being sick for some may not be so far away. In most cases, the children in the catechetical classes should be encouraged to do one thing that will make a difference in the lives of the sick or elderly.

8

HOLY ORDERS

In a day and age when there has been some negative media coverage about Catholic priests, it is important to look at the positive priests who have been a part of the life of the Church. Each person can probably name many holy, caring men who have served the people of God in both positive and difficult circumstances. The Church should be proud of these priests.

What is it that fosters the call to priesthood in a young man? It seems that the single-most influential factor is rooted in a family that values spirituality and service to the Church. Children need to see that their parents respect and value the contribution that a priest makes to a parish or to a ministry in the Church. Parents can encourage their sons to be active in the Church, whether through some organization or as a Mass server. Parents can help their children see that priests are "real" people who have a different calling than they have as married adults.

Theology

Holy orders is the sacrament through which the mission entrusted by Christ to his apostles continues to be exercised in the Church, until the end of time; thus it is the sacrament of apostolic ministry. It includes three degrees: episcopate, presbyterate, and diaconate. (*CCC* 1536). The men in these three degrees are commonly referred to as bishop, priest, and deacon. The sacrament of holy orders creates an indelible mark called a sacramental character on the recipient's soul, just as baptism and confirmation also create this indelible mark.

A bishop is the visible head of the diocese. Bishops are empowered to lead the Church in terms of sound doctrine and pastoral administration.

Priests unite with the bishops in taking care of the pastoral functions within a particular church or office within the diocese. They may administer all of the sacraments except holy orders.

Deacons are called as ministers of service, delegated to act in the name of the Church. Deacons witness marriages (as the sacrament of matrimony is actually conferred by the couple upon each other). Deacons are called to preach, to baptize and to work in areas of pastoral governance and the service of charity.

From the time of the Old Testament, God had called a special tribe (Levi) to serve as priests to the rest of the tribes. This service of the Levites is a prefiguring of the ordained ministry. Everything that the priesthood of the Old Covenant prefigured finds its fulfillment in Christ Jesus. (*CCC* 1544)

In the New Testament, there were a lot of questions about what kind of person to choose as a leader in the early Church. Three pastoral letters (1 and 2 Timothy and Titus) were probably written by Paul's next generation of disciples. The three letters begin by listing the qualities to look for in a good bishop—self-control, hospitality, and gentleness—and in the deacons who would serve with him in ministry. (1 Timothy 3:2–13; 4:7–9) As to the most dangerous temptation leaders must guard against, 1 Timothy is quite clear: "For the love of money is the root of all evils, and some people in their desire for it have strayed from the faith." (1 Timothy 6:10)

The whole Church is a priestly people. Through baptism all the faithful share in the priesthood of Christ. (*CCC* 1591) The ministerial priesthood differs in essence from the common priesthood of the faithful because it confers a sacred power for the service of the faithful. The ordained ministers exercise their service for the people of God by teaching, divine worship, and pastoral governance. (*CCC* 1592)

Catechetical Perspective

The sacrament of holy orders is a sacrament that is a part of the group: "sacraments of service." As a catechist, it is important to stress to the children that this is a special calling, just as being called to the sacrament of matrimony is a special calling in line of service.

While each child in your class has probably attended someone's wedding, it is not as common for a child to have attended a priest's ordination. Therefore it is important to explain the ordination ceremony to the children. It is recommended that the ordination of a bishop, a priest, or a deacon takes place in the context of Sunday liturgy, when the people of the parish and diocese can participate. However, unless the family personally knows one or more of the persons to be ordained, many "ordinary" Catholics don't attend the ordinations. Only a bishop is able to validly confer the sacrament of holy orders.

The ordination to the priesthood is a time of great joy and celebration for the newly ordained priest, his family, and friends, and all those who have encouraged and supported him throughout his years of formation leading up to ordination.

On the day of ordination, the ordinands gather for the Mass dressed in albs and the diagonally worn stoles of deacons. The ordination Mass is often well-attended by many—priests, friends, and family—who show their support for their newest member of the priesthood.

After the opening prayers of the Mass and the Scripture readings, the ordaining bishop calls each priestly candidate by name. The candidate responds with, "Present," and steps forward. The bishop then asks for testimony that the candidates have received proper training and are worthy of ordination. Some religious official attests that the candidates are ready to be ordained. The bishop then accepts the men, and the people gathered usually applaud in approval.

Each candidate then approaches the bishop, and the bishop asks him if he is willing to serve Christ and the Church as a faithful priest. The ordinand then promises obedience to the authority of the Church and to his own religious superiors. The bishop kneels and invites all of those present to join in prayer for the candidates. *The Litany of the Saints* is also chanted at this time, and is quite moving, as the candidates prostrate themselves before the altar during this litany. The litany invokes all the saints as well as God's mercy to send the Holy Spirit upon these men, soon to be ordained.

The most solemn and essential act of the rite follows the litany. It is the moment when the bishop lays his hands upon the head of the ordinand, and prays silently calling the Holy Spirit upon the newly ordained priest. Each of the other priests in attendance at the ordination then lays his hands on the head of the newly ordained priest. This signifies a bond and unity in the brotherhood of priests. It is a visible sign of welcome to the new priest.

At this time the newly ordained priest removes his deacon's stole and is vested in the priestly stole and chasuble. The bishop then anoints the palms of the newly ordained priest with the oil of chrism. The priest's hands are wrapped with a linen cloth.

The Ordination Mass continues with the presentation of the gifts of bread and wine. After the gifts are brought to the altar, the bishop gives the paten and the chalice to the new priest, symbolizing the sacred Body and Blood of Christ in the Eucharist. The rest of the Mass continues as usual, until it is time for the conclusion of the Mass. At that time the newly ordained priest gives his first blessing to the ordaining bishop, followed by the new priest giving his blessing to all of the family and friends present for the celebration.

Following ordination, there is usually a reception with food and drink celebrating the happy event. The next day, the newly ordained priest celebrates his first Mass, with his family and friends again in attendance for this special Mass. This is a Mass of thanksgiving to God for the gift of priesthood.

Family Connection

○ **Send a note to your pastor** thanking him for his service to the parish. If possible, it would be good to invite the pastor to your home for a meal, so that you get better acquainted with him.

○ **Many parishes have a Traveling Chalice,** where a chosen family receives a chalice at Mass time, and for the entire week he or she prays for vocations. The next week the chalice is brought back to Mass and passed on to another family. Get this started in your parish, if it doesn't exist. Or participate in the traveling chalice program, if it does exist.

○ **Go to YouTube** and view one of the ordinations. It probably will not be from your own diocese, but it will give a visual of the ceremony.

CATECHETICAL ACTIVITY NO. 1

Saint Peter Claver is an example of a priest who literally "went the extra mile," as he was a missionary. A missionary is a person who is sent to witness to God and spread the word of God to people who do not yet know God. He was a missionary to black slaves in South America and the West Indies. He is the patron saint of Catholic missions among black people.

Before introducing this activity you may also need to explain the word "mission" which means a place where the Gospel is not yet known. The word "patron saint" may also be new to children. It is a saint to whom one can pray for a particular blessing from God. You might want to ask the children about what other patron saints they have heard (like Saint Patrick, patron saint of Ireland; Saint Anthony, patron saint of lost items; Saint Blaise, patron saint of throats). The medals section of religious goods catalogs is a great place to find saints, or the Internet can help you locate some examples of patron saints. Remind the children that many patron saints, especially those like Saint Peter Claver, took their priestly calling in the sacrament of holy orders to people in other parts of the world.

Note: You will need a world map for this activity and some small circular adhesive bandages.

Gather around the world map that has been placed on a wall or a table. Explain to the children that there are many places in the world where no one knows about God. A missionary goes to these places to teach the people about God. Let's all pretend that we are missionaries. Let's each choose a country that we would like to go to and share God's word.

The children can then go to the world map, and point out places where they would like to go to be a missionary. You can put a small bandage on the map showing that these people are hurting since they do not know God. Be sure to also discuss the fact that in our own country there are many people who do not believe in God. They, too, need to have missionaries share God with them. Remind the children that we need to pray for missionaries in both our own country and in other parts of the world. As a closing prayer for this activity, name off each country or state where a bandage was placed. After each name, have the class say: "Saint Peter Claver, bless this mission."

CATECHETICAL ACTIVITY NO. 2

Take the children on a field trip, by means of the Internet. Go to the website of the United States Conference of Catholic Bishops (www.usccb.org). Have them find information on some of the various ministries within which the bishops participate. Do any of these ministries give opportunities to "give without drawing attention to the giver?" Be sure that as a catechist you have studied the website and perhaps even have written a list of questions to which the children will find the answers.

CATECHETICAL ACTIVITY NO. 3

Take your catechetical class on a field trip to church, with your pastor as the guest speaker. Ask the pastor to show the variety of vestments used at Mass and at other special occasions throughout the year. Have the pastor show the sacred vessels that are also used as a part of liturgy. Lastly, have Father share the story of his vocational calling with the children.

CATECHETICAL ACTIVITY NO. 4

If you have a deacon in your parish, invite the deacon to visit your catechetical class, and explain to the children what he does as a deacon. Work with the children to have some questions prepared for the deacon in advance.

CATECHETICAL ACTIVITY NO. 5

An echo story is a popular catechetical activity for several reasons: There is no memorization of lines by the children, there is a high retention of the story because the children use their bodies as well as their minds to grasp the story, and this technique can be used with all ages of children.

Have the children stand up. Echo stories have the catechist saying a line of the story and putting actions and facial expressions with the words. The children repeat the words, actions, and facial expressions, hence the term "Echo Story."

In this story, the children will become acquainted with Saint Ignatius Loyola, a priest who founded the Jesuits. Ignatius was born

"Inigo" in 1491 in Loyola, Spain. He and other famous saints, such as Saint Francis Xavier, spread the spirituality and education by which the Jesuits are known. Saint Ignatius Loyola died in 1556. His feast is celebrated on July 31, and he is the patron of soldiers, educators, and the Society of Jesus (Jesuits).

Saint Ignatius lived a long time ago.
    (point thumb repeatedly over shoulder on "ago")
But he was a real person like you and me.
    (point to "you" and "me")
He was born in Loyola, Spain, which is far away.
    (hold hand over eyes as if looking far, far away)
He was baptized "Inigo" which means "My Little"
    (bend down, showing the size of a small child)
He was the youngest of thirteen children.
    (count off thirteen on your fingers)
His mother died when he was only seven years old.
    (droop head, close eyes)
When Ignatius grew up,
    (raise hands in increments showing growth)
he became a soldier and rode off to battle.
    (act as if riding a horse)
But his leg was hurt in battle.
    (limp and hold your leg as if it is hurt)
He prayed that his leg would be cured.
    (fold hands in prayer)
But that did not happen.
    (shake head "no")
So he went off to study.
    (raise hands as if holding a book)
One of his roommates was wild,
    (wave arms as if acting wild)

One of his roommates was poor.

(reach in pocket, and show open hand with no money)

Ignatius became friends with both of them,

(open arms widely)

Ignatius taught his friends how to pray.

(fold hands in prayer)

He helped his wild friend to repent.

(make the sign of the cross)

He helped his poor friend get money

(rub fingers together for "money")

…from tutoring students.

(tap head showing smartness)

Ignatius called his friend Francis the "lumpiest dough."

(act like kneading bread dough)

But he didn't give up on him.

(shake head "no")

All the roommates loved God.

(make the sign of the cross)

They knew that God comes first in their lives.

(point toward heaven)

Ignatius traveled by horse

(gallop as if riding a horse)

to many parts of the world.

(turn in a full circle with arms outstretched)

His friend, Francis Xavier, traveled by ship.

(move hands up and down as if riding waves)

On the ship, the food rotted.

(hold nose, as if smelling rotten food)

Many people got sick.

(hold stomach, as if sick)

But Francis Xavier rolled up his sleeves and took care of them.

(roll up sleeves)

He knew that God comes first in his life.

(point toward heaven)

Ignatius loved God most of all.

(draw heart on chest)

He thought he might want to be a priest,

(bless the group)

and was so surprised!

(slap cheeks with hands)

Could he be called to do something so important?

(cup ear, as if to hear)

Could his friends be called to do something so important?

(cup ear, as if to hear)

God wanted Ignatius and his friends

(count off three fingers for three friends)

to start a group of priests called the Jesuits.

(make the sign of the cross)

He was so surprised!

(slap cheeks with hands)

They knew that God comes first in their lives.

(point toward heaven)

They served as missionaries.

(turn in full circle with arms outstretched)

They served as teachers.

(raise hands as if holding a book)

They helped other people to pray.

(make the sign of the cross)

Because they knew that God should come first in their lives.

(give the No. 1 sign with finger)

(in softer voice) God should come first in our lives.

(give the No. 1 sign with finger again)

(in whisper) God should come first in our lives.

(give the No. 1 sign with finger again)

QUESTIONS FOR DISCUSSION

Let the children sit down.

Discuss the various ministries of priests (missionary, educator, pastor, retreat director, for examples)

Explain the difference between a "diocesan" or "secular" priest and a "religious" priest, such as a Jesuit or Franciscan. Essentially what makes a "religious" different from a "secular" is that the secular priests never take the three vows of religion: poverty, chastity, and obedience. They do make a promise to their bishop at ordination to obey him as their spiritual leader for a particular diocese, and they also make a promise to remain celibate—not to marry. The promise of celibacy is not the same as the vow of chastity.

Ask whether they know anyone who wants to become a priest. If you have a seminarian in your parish, you could invite the seminarian to come to class and share his vocational call with the children. If you do not have a seminarian, you could invite a priest to come and share his vocational call.

Concluding Remarks

The words of Scripture are like seeds that, when given the right environment, can grow and bear fruit. In Matthew 19:21, Jesus tells a young man that "if you wish to be perfect, go, sell what you have and give to the poor, and you will have treasure in heaven. Then come, follow me."

Although everyone hearing these words of Jesus do not follow the command, there are those men who do. The priests in the Catholic Church make huge sacrifices to be the servants of God. They will get their treasure in heaven. How many of the children in the catechetical programs will take up this challenge from Jesus?

9

MATRIMONY

There is a popular children's game called "telephone" in which a message is whispered from person to person until the end of the line. Usually the message is fairly complicated, and as it gets passed from person to person, the details often get confused. The last person to hear the message says it out loud, and it is compared to the message of the first person. Most often the last message has very little resemblance to the first message. This is a great choice of game to play with couples preparing for marriage. Why would one play a children's game with adults? Communication and listening skills are key elements to a successful marriage, and this game vividly illustrates what happens when good communication is not practiced.

In marriage, each spouse needs to pay close attention not only to the words of the partner but also to the body language that will tell the full story. It is important to get rid of distractions, attitudes, and attachments that could hinder listening to the other.

A marriage doesn't easily last for a lifetime. There are times when each member wants to give it up. Compatibility on the day of the wedding is no guarantee for happily ever after. The couple consciously and deliberately work at the marriage, if it is to last a lifetime. Only with this hard work is the true vocation revealed and the many graces of God bestowed.

Theology

The sacrament of matrimony was the last of the seven sacraments to be named by the Church, as it was more than a thousand years after Jesus' death before it was listed as a sacrament. Why did it take so long? It is suggested that the Church considered marriage to be tied to creation. Marriage traces its history back to the Garden of Eden, where humans were created in the image of God, male and female. Marriage was considered ordinary and not of sacramental nature. Marriage was around long before Jesus.

"The marriage covenant, by which a man and a woman form with each other an intimate communion of life and love, has been founded and endowed with its own special laws by the Creator. By its very nature, it is ordered to the good of the couple, as well as to the generation and education of children. Christ the Lord raised marriage between the baptized to the dignity of a sacrament." (*CCC* 1660)

The Church gradually began to think of marriage as a sacramental reality. It was obvious that there was great joy in creating and raising children. There was also great joy in love between a husband and wife. The Church gradually began to appreciate the experience of marital love, especially in nurturing children. Religious rituals and codes of behavior have always been a part of marriage. In the Middle Ages (700 to 1400), the Church became more involved in the legal structures of society. Eventually the Church officially witnessed marriages between Christians and realized that there was something special about the marriage between a husband and wife. The Council of Trent in the sixteenth century listed Christian marriage as one of the seven sacraments.

We find in the Bible that marriage is somewhat commonplace. Mary and Joseph were married, and we hear about Peter's mother-in-law, so we presume Peter was married.

Several Scripture readings are particularly tied to marital love. The first of these is the story of the wedding feast at Cana. The second is a passage from the Gospel of Matthew. The third significant reading is the Letter of Saint Paul to the Ephesians in which Saint Paul describes marriage as part of the relationship between Jesus and the Church.

The story of Cana is a wonderful example of Jesus' love of his mother and of his concern for the feelings of his friends. Each of us has been to a wedding reception where the bride and groom overspent in an effort to have their family and friends have a great time. Weddings in the time of Jesus were probably no different. The newly married couple at Cana thought they had purchased enough wine to last throughout the celebration, and instead they were running out of wine before the end of the party. Mary, like many caring women, noticed first that the wine was running out. She mentioned the fact to her son because she knew he could do something about it. His response gives us the sense that he wasn't too eager to do what his mother wanted. Perhaps he didn't think that it was time for his miracle. Yet, like a good son, Jesus ultimately does what his mother wants and saves the newly married couple from embarrassment. This first miracle was part of God's plan, and God chose a wedding as the site of the miracle.

In the Gospel of Matthew, Jesus gives instruction to the Pharisees: "Have you not read that from the beginning the Creator 'made them male and female' and said, 'For this reason a man shall leave his father and mother and be joined to his wife, and the two shall become one flesh'? So they are no longer two, but one flesh. Therefore, what God has joined together, no human being must separate." (Matthew 19:4–7)

In Saint Paul's Letter to the Ephesians, the description between God and God's people is in terms of marriage: "For this reason a man shall leave (his) father and (his) mother and be joined to his wife, and the two shall become one flesh. This is a great mystery, but I speak in reference to Christ and the church."(Ephesians 5:31–32) Matrimony is a sacramental vocation in and for the Church. Through matrimony, Christ reveals and deepens the mystery of his oneness with us, the body of Christ. In Ephesians 5:21, husbands and wives are told to "be subordinate to one another out of reverence for Christ." If husbands and wives follow this advice, they truly live a sacramental life. This union is exclusive and indissoluble.

"From a valid marriage arises a bond between the spouses which by its very nature is perpetual and exclusive; furthermore, in a Christian marriage the spouses are strengthened and, as it were, consecrated for the duties and the dignity of their state by a special sacrament." (*CCC* 1638)

The marriage bond between baptized persons can never be dissolved, as long as it has resulted from a free act of the spouses and their consummation of the marriage. In some very difficult situations, the couple may need to separate physically. This does not mean that they are no longer married to each other in the eyes of the Church. Therefore they are not free to marry other people.

In the current environment, the divorce rate is one of the highest in history. Numerous Catholics have resorted to civil divorce and new civil unions. The Church does not recognize this new union, unless the first marriage has been deemed as invalid. An annulment of the first union would need to take place before the new union could be validated in the Church. A Church annulment is an official decision by the Church that the previous marriage was not valid from the beginning of the marriage. This does not affect the legitimacy of the children that the couple may have had.

The Church has come to regard marital fidelity as a sign of God's fidelity to us. Just as God has entered a covenantal bond marked by perseverance and commitment without end, so does the covenant of marriage, in its way, reflect this aspect of God.

Catechetical Perspective

Marriage is one sacrament that is not performed by a priest or bishop. It is the bride and groom who perform the marriage. The priest, the attendants, and the community witness what the bride and groom do as they pronounce their vows. This may be a new teaching for many children in our catechetical classes.

The couple can say traditional vows on their own or they can repeat after the priest. The bride and groom can write non-traditional vows for themselves. One such marriage vow could be, "Today I commit my body and spirit to you. I promise to try always to make our relationship grow through openness in communication, through trust in your willingness to work toward our mutual good; through faith in our love for each other even when that love seems hidden for the moment. Today I promise you the freedom to grow and change and develop your talents and capabilities. I promise to rejoice in your personal growth and to work out with you any problems this growth or change entails. Today I pledge to join with you in a union that is meant to be fruitful. I promise to accept any children with which we are blessed. I promise to join with you in establishing a household that is open to the needs of others, where we can, so far as we are able, provide a place of warmth and belonging to those who have none."

Three important elements in this vow reflect three important aspects of marriage: commitment to each other, personal freedom to grow and change, and fruitfulness. Marriage is a covenant between the spouses that commits them to the well-being of each other and the procreation and upbringing of children.

How can we make a lifelong commitment when we have no idea what the future will bring? The sacrament of matrimony imparts special graces on the day of the marriage. As the newly married couple leaves the altar after the ceremony, their souls are spiritually stronger than they were when they came to the altar. However, that is not the end of the graces. The sacrament imparts special graces throughout the lifetime of the marriage. As the couple continually reaffirms their commitment to each other, they acknowledge, draw upon and witness to the presence and power of graces within their lives. Christ has pledged these graces to the couple to draw upon when there is a bad day, or when extra strength is needed to remain faithful to their vows. This can happen when there is an illness in the family, when there is financial stress, or when bad things just seem to happen.

In discussing marriage with the children in your class, it is important to talk about some things that can strengthen a marriage. Most of the children in your class will choose this vocation, and that is the context in which you can approach these steps. They probably observe many of these things within their homes, for better or worse, but it may be helpful to put these strengths in the context of a child's best friend.

Adult example: When times get tough in a marriage, remember why you married your partner. No matter how good the marriage is, there will be tough times that will need to be worked through together.

Child example: When you have an argument with your best friend, remember why you are best friends. Think of the good times when you and your friend stuck by each other.

Adult example: Treat your spouse with respect. Once children come along, this respect of each other is observed each day.

Child example: Treat your best friend with respect. Don't let other people make fun of your friend.

Adult example: Get used to not having your way all the time. Be willing to give in to your spouse.

Child example: Get used to not having your way all the time. If your best friend wants to play a certain game and you don't, be willing to give in and do what your friend wants you to do.

Adult example: Make it a daily habit to tell your spouse why you love him or her. See how many different reasons you can find.

Child example: Tell your best friend why you like him or her. See how many different reasons you can find. Is he fun to be around? Is he kind to others?

Adult example: Make time to show affection each day to your spouse. If your spouse is out of town, figure out a way to still show "affection" by your phone call, a note in the suitcase, or some other way.

Child example: If your best friend is sick, do you make her a get-well card, or go to visit her? If your best friend needs to be cheered up, what do you do to make her feel better?

Adult example: Make your needs and expectations known clearly. People don't always get hints, so speak clearly.

Child example: Sometimes you talk in "circles" with your best friend. If your friend asks you a question, answer the question honestly and completely.

Adult example: Enjoy sexual desire and intimacy with your spouse. According to research, couples with an active and happy sex life live longer and are happier in other aspects of life.

Child example: This one is hard to compare to the adult example. There are positive feelings, however, just from having friends.

Adult example: Keep the spark alive. Don't get in a rut. Continue to work at keeping a vibrant marriage.

Child example: It is important, even in friendship among children, to try to pay attention to what would make your friend happy. When your friend needs a listening ear, are you there for him? When your friend needs someone to stand by him, do you speak up for your friend?

It is also important in your class to be non-judgmental of the children's parents, who may or may not be living in a Catholic marriage. Both the priests and the parish community are encouraged to cultivate an atmosphere of acceptance and encouragement of these spouses. The families should be encouraged to attend Mass and stay active in the parish through works of charity and times of prayer. The families are also encouraged to educate their children in the Catholic faith.

The family home is called the "domestic church" because it is the first place where children learn their faith. It is a community of faith, hope, and love and is the place where spiritual and moral values are learned. The best thing that parents can do for their children is to love each other and to let this love permeate the entire home. Members of the family should learn to care for each other and to respect each other. This same care and respect will then be shared with the larger community where they live.

Family Connection

○ **Ordinary places and times**, such as weddings, have been the site of miracles for Jesus. Share with your child times when you have seen a "miracle" and talk about whether or not this was a part of an ordinary place and time.

○ **Show your child pictures** of your own wedding. Who was in the wedding party? Did you have a reception? What do you recall about the vows that you exchanged? Did you write your own or use traditional vows? What was most special about your day?

○ **Encourage your children to celebrate** your wedding anniversary in a special way. Smaller children can pick flowers for you, or make cards and decorate the house for you. Older children could fix a special meal or dessert.

○ **Have each child make a place mat** that could be used on your family dinner table. Suggest that your child draw a picture or put words on the place mat that celebrate the idea of your marriage as husband and wife and as a family.

○ **As a family,** choose a way to share with persons who are not as fortunate. This often happens at Christmas but could be incorporated at other times of the year as well. If you have the money to share, that is fine. If you do not have money to share, know that there are gifts of time that can be shared with others.

CATECHETICAL ACTIVITY NO. 1

Bring the following items to class: flowers, ring, and a picture of a wedding gown. Discuss with the children these various symbols of marriage:

The bouquet of flowers carried by the bride is an ancient symbol of fertility and a call for protection upon the new couple.

The rings symbolize continuity and that marriage is to last forever.

The white wedding gown is a reminder of the white baptismal gown worn by the child for baptism.

CATECHETICAL ACTIVITY NO. 2

If you are working with older children, have them write the marriage vows that a bride and groom could exchange on their wedding day. Discuss the kind of elements that would be important in the vows.

CATECHETICAL ACTIVITY NO. 3

Bring into class several CDs containing popular love songs. Discuss with the class whether the love described in the song demonstrates a sacramental love or if it is a self-centered love in which each man and woman is out for his or her own satisfaction.

CATECHETICAL ACTIVITY NO. 4

Make five-by-seven-inch signs of each name of Biblical couples. For example, Adam and Eve, Abraham and Sarah, Isaac and Rebecca, Boaz and Ruth, Joseph and Mary, and Zechariah and Elizabeth. Give each student one of the signs, and pin it on his or her back. Have the student show the class the name on his or her back. Have the student ask questions of the entire class until the student can guess whose name is on his or her back, based on the answers that the class gives.

If you are working with older students who know these biblical couples very well, you may want to have them walk around the room with the name pinned to his or her back. They can ask questions of individuals within the class, instead of asking the entire class.

CATECHETICAL ACTIVITY NO. 5

Invite a guest speaker to your class. This speaker could be someone who works with marriage preparation in the parish. Prepare questions in advance to find out what the speaker does to help young couples prepare for marriage.

CATECHETICAL ACTIVITY NO. 6

As an outside assignment, have the children interview three married couples, asking the couples to tell two or three things they do to keep their marriage happy. If you are working with older children, you can also include questions about the tough times within a marriage. Prepare the questions through discussion in class.

Concluding Remarks

When the bishops of the United States released their pastoral letter titled "Marriage: Love and Life in the Divine Plan" they put forth a blueprint for marriage that would encourage and inspire couples at any stage of their lives. One of the major themes flowing through this document was that each home was to be a mini-church. The home was to be a place where each family member was to experience Jesus' love and where that love was the basis of life in that home.

Encourage the children in your catechetical classes to support their parents in making the home this mini-church. Help them to establish a common philosophy and goals that could unite the family as an environment where everyone enjoys being together. Encourage everyone to work together for the good of the family. Kindness, sincerity, and love are values that create a peaceful home, and they will foster a strong faith life.

10

TEMPLATES AND GUIDELINES FOR ACTIVITIES

Where do you begin in getting fun, creative activities to use in your religion class? Here are some ideas:

Your religion textbook should have some activities. Don't feel you need to be glued to each page of the textbook. Take an activity and adapt it to be more entertaining.

Magazines and professional journals that are geared to teaching religion, whether in a Catholic school or in a parish setting, offer great articles with creative ideas. Read an idea and see if it fits your particular class, or if you need to make some adaptation.

Games that are on TV or that exist as board games are fun ideas that the students already know how to play and can be adapted to your particular content.

Other catechists can share ideas with you. Ask your director of religious education or your principal to hold sharing sessions of ideas at least two or three times a year. If your group is large enough, you can break into grade-sectionals. Otherwise, listen for good ideas and then change the idea to meet your age level of student and your content.

Gather your ideas in a file on the computer or in your home. File them according to themes or topics. It doesn't matter what age level the activity is originally aimed at, because most activities can be adapted to fit the age of your students. It may mean that you have to write some words on a board or that you have to practice ahead of doing the actual activity. In the end, it is well worth it to have the students participating in an engaging activity.

A child remembers:

- ○ twenty percent of what he hears
- ○ thirty percent of what he sees
- ○ fifty percent of what he hears and sees
- ○ seventy percent of what he says
- ○ ninety percent of what he does

Is there any question about how a catechist needs to structure her lesson plan? A lesson plan is like a road map containing a number of routes, any one of which may be appropriate on a given day with a particular group. The lesson plan that you used last year with this same age level may not work as well this year with the new class of students. Each group is different!

The best way to teach is through creative, exciting learning activities. Several principles help guide that teaching:

Each person in the class should be a part of the learning process. Everyone should be paying attention to whatever is being done in the activity. Try to involve the entire class in some way.

Understand how to engage the class during the activity. Know the activity very well so that you as catechist can adapt anything that should come up during the class. Be prepared for anything.

Activities should be planned so that each person enjoys the activity and feels successful in his part in the activity. Cooperative learning is the mode of operation. Smile, laugh, and enjoy the interaction and creativity of the students.

One danger associated with lesson planning is a tendency of beginning teachers to stick too rigidly to a plan. Do not feel duty-bound to cover every point in the exact order, no matter what.

However, do not teach without a lesson plan. Prepare in advance all the materials that you need for the lesson. Be sure to incorporate activities that will have the student *doing*, and not just hearing. Nothing is more boring than a predictable lesson. Get the students up and moving.

Prepare alternate approaches to the same lesson. If one approach fails, switch quickly.

Determine the attention span of your students. Vary your presentations, activities, and methods frequently enough during the course of the lesson to meet the needs of your students. Age does not determine attention span, necessarily. The time of day when the class is held can affect the attention span.

There is no one correct way of teaching a lesson. The approach you choose must be comfortable for you and your students. Evaluate each lesson after the session. Adjust your plans for the next session according to your honest assessment of the lesson plan.

Tasks of Catechesis

As you prepare each of your lessons for catechizing the children, you can remember that there are certain tasks/objectives of catechesis. These were outlined in the *General Directory of Catechesis (GDC)*. The six tasks of catechesis are first seen in the mission of Christ. He taught his disciples to pray, he inculcated in them the gospel virtues, and he prepared them to bring the Gospel to others. That is the overall objective for each catechist, as well.

1. The first task of catechesis is to **promote knowledge of the faith**. The student, having come to a first knowledge of Christ, desires to know him more and more through the study of tradition and the Scriptures. This task is the deepening of the understanding of the profession of faith or creed. The deeper knowledge of the faith not only helps the student live more

fully in Christ but also prepares her to give an account of the faith to others. The specific content geared to this first task is determined by the content of your grade level.

2. In the second task, catechesis must **lead to full, conscious and active participation in the sacred liturgy**. Through catechesis, the student is educated in the most privileged encounters we have with Christ in the Church: the sacred liturgy, especially the sacraments. Some grade levels focus on the sacraments more than others, but all grades should include some catechesis on sacraments in general, and certainly all grades will include lessons on the liturgy.

3. The third task of catechesis is to give **moral formation**. Knowledge of Christ necessarily entails accompanying Christ along the Way of the Cross. Catechesis prepares the student to witness to Christ in the manner of his daily living. The Sermon on the Mount, by which Christ teaches the full meaning of the Ten Commandments, is the constant point of reference for catechesis in providing moral formation. The student needs to see that the way in which he lives is as important as what he believes. Living and believing are entwined.

4. The fourth task is that catechesis must **teach students how to pray**. Deeper friendship with Jesus Christ means praying with him, especially in the words which he himself has taught us: the Our Father. All of the sentiments, which Our Lord Jesus expresses in the Our Father, are taught in catechesis. Every class should include prayer, and there should be specific lessons helping the students to learn the many forms of prayer.

5. In the fifth task, catechesis must **educate students for community life**. Catechesis inculcates in the student the virtues, which foster the life of the Church: the concern and care for others in the community. Education for community life inspires the desire of Christian unity. Catechesis promotes true ecumenism

to the degree that it provides the student with a full and clear presentation of the Church's teaching.

6. The final task of catechesis **provides initiation into the mission**. Catechesis prepares the student to be an effective witness of Jesus Christ in the world. At the same time, it introduces the student into direct service of the Church, in accord with whatever vocation in life she will choose.

In introducing the student into the mission of the Church, catechesis should foster very much the vocations to the ordained priesthood and to the consecrated life in its various forms. This will enable the student whom God is calling to these vocations to be assisted in responding for the building-up of the Body of Christ.

The presentation of the Church's teaching should include the elements of faith, which the Catholic Church shares with other Christian churches and ecclesial communities. This mission includes preparation for respectful conversation with persons of other religions, for example, Judaism or Islam.

Activities for Catechesis

Whether trying to incorporate one of the tasks of catechesis specifically into your lesson plan, or in just trying to follow a prepared lesson plan, these are activities that could be included to "spice up" the class. Use a variety of these activities, in order to keep your classes interesting to the students.

Plays

Make the Scripture or story into a play where student "actors" and "actresses" present the story as a drama. To make it even more interesting, assign a story or situation from the lesson to groups of children. Have them act out the story charades-style and see if the other groups can guess the correct story or situation.

Games

Often you can create a game that makes the point to the lesson of that day. It is easiest for the students if you use a game with which they are familiar.

For example, put together games such as Jeopardy, Bingo, or Family Feud using the content from that week's lesson.

For the categories game, have the children write the letters of the alphabet down the left side of the paper. Challenge them to write a word to describe the category beginning with each letter of the alphabet.

A variation on this is to have the children write a category word from the lesson down the left side of the paper and then write a word defining the category. The definition words need to fit the lesson.

Music

Play a song or teach a song to your class that relates to the message of your lesson. Most young students love to sing a song, while the older students prefer to listen to a song.

Another way to incorporate music is to take a theme or Scripture story and put it into an original song or rap. Perform this original piece for the rest of the class.

Tell a Story

Storytelling is a powerful tool within a lesson. Stories evoke enthusiastic response. Don't read the story. Tell it. Some of the skills needed to be a good storyteller come naturally, but you can learn how to be a good storyteller.

Make your point by telling a story from your life. Students like to know about you. If storytelling is difficult for you, practice. It does get easier.

When you tell a story to your class, arrange the students so that you can have eye contact with each of them. Speak in a comfortable tone of voice. Use your voice to bring the words alive. See the story in your mind. Describe all the details you see. You are creating a new world.

Arts and Crafts

A twig cross is a traditional craft project. For this craft, each child needs two twigs. The best twigs would be one thick twig about ten inches long and a thinner twig about seven inches long.

Have the students lay the shorter twig across the longer piece as a crossbar. Provide green yarn. Demonstrate how to wrap the yarn around the twigs where they intersect.

Give each child a small spray of white silk flowers that can be purchased inexpensively at craft stores. Use green yarn to attach the flowers in the same manner as before. Cut the excess yarn close to the cross.

These crosses can be taken home and displayed as a reminder of God's love. Jesus was willing to die on the cross for us, and most importantly, to be raised from the dead for us.

Interviews

Students can research information about a biblical character, saint or historical character. One student will act as a reporter and interview the other student, who answers questions in the role of the character. To explain this activity to students, use the example of a popular talk-show host on TV. The age of the students will determine how much help they will need for this activity. It may be better for the catechist or an aide to take the part of the reporter, as it is often difficult for children to ask probing questions.

Younger children could also do interviews or "on-the-scene" news broadcasts, acting like a character within a Scripture story. Imagine cameras tracking every minute of the event as it unfolds, with an anchor news person giving live updates and interviewing the key characters.

Kids love to welcome visitors to class. The students can interview guest speakers as they share their experience with the students. The speaker's stories may open the students' eyes to the importance of the day's topic. For example, when teaching the sacrament of the anointing of the sick, invite a minister of care from the parish, one who goes to the nursing homes or hospitals to visit the sick and elderly. When you invite speakers, ask them to bring photographs, videos or DVDs that illustrate the ministry. You could also invite the speaker to bring any object along to the class that they use in the ministry. For example, for the anointing of the sick the minister could bring the oil that is used in the anointing of the sick.

Ask your guest to spend about ten minutes of presentation followed by ten minutes of question time. Ask your guest to not come at the beginning of class, so that you have time as the catechist to prepare the students for the guest. This also allows time to prepare a list of questions for the speaker.

Parables

Jesus' favorite method of teaching was the use of parables. Choose one of the parables from the Bible and have the children give one of two responses to each line of the parable that you read. The two responses are "Right" or "Sorry." Be sure to practice the responses in advance, encouraging the students to be dramatic as they say their responses. If you are working with younger children, you could have signs made with the two responses, so that a leader holds up the proper sign for each line of the parable.

An example of this activity follows:

The Parable of the Wedding Banquet
(Matthew 22:1–14)

Jesus began to address the chief priests and elders of the people once more in parables.

"The kingdom of heaven may be likened to a king who gave a wedding feast for his son." (RIGHT)

The king dispatched his servants to summon the invited guests to the wedding, but they refused to come. (SORRY)

The king then dispatched his son to summon the invited guests to the wedding. (RIGHT)

"Tell those invited: 'Behold, I have prepared my banquet, my calves and fattened cattle are killed, and everything is ready; come to the feast.'" (RIGHT)

Some ignored the invitation and went their way. (RIGHT)

One to his farm. (RIGHT)

Another to his business. (RIGHT)

The rest insulted the king's son and killed him. (SORRY)

At this the king grew furious and sent his army to destroy those murderers and burn their city. (RIGHT)

Then the king said, "The banquet is ready, but those who were invited were not worthy to come." (RIGHT)

That is the reason you must go out into the highways and roads and invite to the wedding anyone you can find. (RIGHT)

The servants then went out and rounded up everyone they met. This filled the wedding hall with guests. (RIGHT)

When the king came in to meet the guests, however, he caught sight of a man not properly dressed for a wedding feast. (RIGHT)

The king asked the man how it was that he came not properly dressed. (RIGHT)

The man had nothing to say. (RIGHT)

The king then told the guards "Bind his hands and feet, and

cast him into the darkness outside, where there will be wailing and grinding of teeth." (RIGHT)

CATECHETICAL ACTIVITY NO. 1

Have on hand a gift bag of common items that you can find in your home. Some suggested ones could include a safety pin, an artificial flower, a coin, a balloon, a packet of instant coffee, a birthday candle, a light bulb, and a button. Ask each student to pick an item out of the bag. Using the object each picked, have her write a modern-day Kingdom of God parable.

Examples: God is like a packet of coffee because God gives me a great start to the morning. God is like a button because God holds me together. God is like a light bulb because God lights up my life.

This parable exercise provides an opportunity to discuss the various images of God and to consider how to start looking for God in everyday things.

You could also ask students to bring an item from home and come prepared to share how this item reminds them of God.

CATECHETICAL ACTIVITY NO. 2

Give each member of the class a Tootsie Roll Pop (TRP). Share some of the ideas as follows:

Just as the TRP has a wrapper on it to protect it from getting dirty, having people touch it, getting wet and melting, etc., we often "wrap" ourselves in things to protect us from being hurt, being insulted, being misunderstood, etc. Think about the things in your life that might be your wrapper.

Now take the wrapper off the TRP. What do you do with a TRP? Lick it, and bite it? How long does it last? The outer shell is hard and sweet. It comes in many flavors. Many times our life is like the outer shell. We have wrapped ourselves to protect us from hurts. The outer shell we show to the world is one that is sweet but hard. We have not let go of the things that make us hard. And, like the flavors of the TRP, our outer shell comes in many varieties.

Some people bite the outer shell to get right to the core. Some people are able to recognize what they need to do to find what is inside them right away. Other people are like those who slowly lick the outer shell of the TRP. They take a long time to get to what is inside. They slowly work their way to the middle, little by little. Once the outer shell is gone, in the center is the chewy core attached firmly to the stick. When we let go of our wrapping and outer shell, there is the center where we find the core of our life. The center of the TRP is the love of God, our faith in God, etc. What can you do to finish your outer shell and get to the center of your personal TRP?

CATECHETICAL ACTIVITY NO. 3

After studying the sacraments, use panels of white paper to create a seven-part mural that depicts the reception of each sacrament or symbol for each sacrament. The students can do this mural as a team project and could share it with students of another class. The mural could also be displayed in the narthex of the church or in the activity center of the parish.

CATECHETICAL ACTIVITY NO. 4

After teaching each of the sacraments, have the students make a word-find, word scramble, or crossword puzzle using vocabulary words that were taught during the study of the sacraments.

An example of how to create the word scramble is to write the vocabulary words on individual pieces of paper, one for each student in class. Have the children mix up the letters in the word. The children then take turns writing their mixed-up words on the board or on a large sheet of paper. The rest of the class guesses what the word is. After the correct word is guessed, review the concept of the word. Example: TRACMEASN = SACRAMENT For the review, ask questions such as, "How many sacraments are there? What is the first sacrament we receive?"

CATECHETICAL ACTIVITY NO. 5

Look at a list of careers and professions, for example, biologist, lawyer, nurse, trash collector, parent, writer, electrician, police officer, or teacher. Explain how each can be an expression of one's Catholic faith. What is one thing that a person of each profession listed could do that would identify her as a Catholic to a stranger?

Concluding Remarks

Each day, somewhere in this world, a student thinks about the impact that a former teacher had on his or her life. Helping faith to come alive for a child is both a responsibility and a joy. As a catechist, embrace the moment. Making a difference is the essence of catechesis. You only have one chance with your students. Make it the best. Be the best.

BIBLIOGRAPHY

100 Activities Based on the Catechism of the Catholic Church, by Ellen Rossini (Ignatius Press)

100 Creative Teaching Techniques for Religion Teachers, by Phyllis Vos Wezeman (Twenty-Third Publications)

100 Fun Ways to Livelier Lessons, by Maxine Inkel, SL (Twenty-Third Publications)

Big Book of Ideas for Children's Faith Formation, edited by Beth Branigan McNamara (Our Sunday Visitor, Inc.)

Catechism of the Catholic Church for the United States of America (English translation) copyright © 1994, United States Catholic Conference, Inc.—Libreria Editrice Vaticana. English translation of the Catechism of the Catholic Church: Modifications from the Editio Typica copyright © 1997, United States Catholic Conference, Inc.—Libreria Editrice Vaticana.

Catholic Family, Catholic Home, by Mary Kathleen Glavich, SND (Twenty-Third Publications)

Code of Canon Law, copyright © 1983 Libreria Editrice Vaticana.

Crafting Faith, by Laurine M. Easton (Loyola Press)

Draw and Tell Sacraments, by Julie A. Petras (Our Sunday Visitor, Inc)

Echo Stories for Children, by Page McKean Zyromski (Twenty-Third Publications)

Exploring the Sacraments, by Francine M. O'Connor (Hi-Time Pflaum)

General Directory for Catechesis, by Congregation for the Clergy (Washington, D.C.: United States Conference of Catholic Bishops, 1998), copyright © 1997 Libreria Editrice Vaticana.

In My Heart Room, by Mary Terese Donze, ASC (Liguori Publications)

Leading Students into Scripture, by Mary Kathleen Glavich, SND (Twenty-Third Publications)

Let's Pray—Catholic Prayers and the Mass, by Francine M. O'Connor (Hi-Time Pflaum)

National Directory for Catechesis, copyright © 2005 United States Conference of Catholic Bishops (USCCB), Washington, D.C. All rights reserved.

English translation, original texts, arrangement, and design of *Pastoral Care of the Sick: Rites of Anointing and Viaticum,* © 1982, International Committee on English in the Liturgy (ICEL).

English translation of *Rite of Baptism for Children,* © 1969, ICEL.

English translation of *Rite of Confirmation, Rite of the Blessings of Oils, Rite of Consecrating the Chrism,* © 1972, ICEL.

Teach Me About the Mass, by Paul S. Plum and Joan E. Plum (Our Sunday Visitor, Inc.)

Teach It: Eucharist and the Mass, by Joseph D. White and Ana Arista White (Our Sunday Visitor, Inc.)

The Big Book of Catholic Customs and Traditions for Children's Faith Formation, edited by Beth Branigan McNamara (Our Sunday Visitor, Inc.)

The Saints: 21 Models for Good Living, by Francine M. O'Connor (Hi-Time Pflaum)

The Seven Sacraments, by Sister Mary Fearon, RSM (E.T. Nedder Publishing)

We Worship and Pray, by Francine M. O'Connor (Hi-Time Pflaum)